'Far too often, adults with autism and their experiences seem to be ignored or misunderstood. This book is refreshingly different, bringing interesting new perspectives to the under-explored area of sensory issues in adults. It is written in a way that makes complex topics accessible and, perhaps more importantly, conveys a sense of respect for adults on the spectrum (which is sorely lacking in many texts!). A must-read for adults on the spectrum and those who support them.'

– *Kirsten Hurley, Programme Coordinator,*
Autism Studies, University College Cork

'Diarmuid has had one of the biggest impacts on my life. Having Asperger's has affected me in different ways, ranging from the sensory aspects to the social aspects. My life has completely changed for the better, and the help I have received from Diarmuid has been outstanding. I would recommend this book for anyone on the autism spectrum.'

– *Cian Hutt, student with Asperger's syndrome*

of related interest

Sensory Perceptual Issues in Autism and Asperger Syndrome
Second Edition
Different Sensory Experiences – Different Perceptual Worlds
Olga Bogdashina
Foreword by Manuel Casanova
ISBN 978 1 84905 673 1
eISBN 978 1 78450 179 2

Older Adults and Autism Spectrum Conditions
An Introduction and Guide
Wenn Lawson
Foreword by Carol Povey
ISBN 978 1 84905 961 9
eISBN 978 0 85700 813 8

**Marriage and Lasting Relationships with Asperger's Syndrome
(Autism Spectrum Disorder)**
Successful Strategies for Couples or Counselors
Eva A. Mendes
Foreword by Stephen M. Shore
ISBN 978 1 84905 999 2
eISBN 978 0 85700 981 4

Life on the Autism Spectrum – A Guide for Girls and Women
Karen McKibbin
Foreword by Tony Attwood
ISBN 978 1 84905 747 9
eISBN 978 1 78450 193 8

SENSORY ISSUES

FOR ADULTS WITH

AUTISM
SPECTRUM
DISORDER

DIARMUID HEFFERNAN

Jessica Kingsley *Publishers*
London and Philadelphia

First published in 2016
by Jessica Kingsley Publishers
73 Collier Street
London N1 9BE, UK
and
400 Market Street, Suite 400
Philadelphia, PA 19106, USA

www.jkp.com

Library of Congress Cataloging in Publication Data
Heffernan, Diarmuid.
  Sensory issues for adults with autism spectrum disorder / Diarmuid
Heffernan.
     pages cm
  Includes bibliographical references and index.
  ISBN 978-1-84905-661-8 (alk. paper)
  1. Autism spectrum disorders. 2. Perceptual disorders. I. Title.
  RC553.A88H44 2016
  616.85'882--dc23
                                        2015031395

British Library Cataloguing in Publication Data
A CIP catalogue record for this book is available from the British Library

ISBN 978 1 84905 661 8
eISBN 978 1 78450 212 6

CONTENTS

FOREWORD

Dr Luke Beardon

It was about twenty years ago that I became obsessively fascinated around the sensory differences experienced by people with autism, after having met an individual for whom the feeling of drops of water on his skin was intolerable. Finally, in 2013, DSM-5 included sensory processing in the diagnostic criteria. And yet, in the main, the world of sensory processing remains one which does not have the level of exploration that is required in order to best understand the autistic experience. Some authors, notably Olga Bogdashina and Brenda Smith Myles, have gone a long way towards advancing knowledge in this area; Diarmuid has added to the literature with his rich, in depth, accessible book which is full of beneficial information for people with autism, families, and professionals.

It is incredibly difficult, unless one experiences sensory differences oneself, to appreciate just how impactful the sensory world can be. For many people with autism, it is the sensory reality that can so often impinge on how they live their lives. Many individuals will report that their way of perceiving the sensory world - both in a positive and negative way - leads to an array of behaviour that is frequently misunderstood. Without an intuitively empathic way of understanding sensory profiles, anyone involved with an autistic individual who is influenced by the sensory environment will need some other way of appreciating the autistic experience. Sometimes, the individual (him/herself) will be the best person to develop understanding. At other times, however, it may be necessary to look elsewhere.

In his book, Diarmuid manages to explain what is a hugely complicated subject area in a way that is eminently readable and informative. He bridges the gap between science and the lived experience extremely well, with a healthy dose of suggested ways in which individuals might be supported.

I frequently meet individuals who report their sensory experiences fantastically well, enabling me to accept why it might be so problematic to walk down a busy street, or have a hug, or wear a certain colour of clothes (the list, while not endless, could go on, and on); this does not mean I have a genuine understanding of these things, but at least knowledge of them helps me to accept them. While Diarmuid's book also explores the myriad of ways an autistic person might experience the world, he also provides some excellent theory, which supports his rationales and real life examples.

I am as obsessed now as I was those two decades ago, so I was full of excited anticipation when asked to read Diarmuid's book and write a foreword. I am very pleased that my excitement was well justified; this is an excellent read, and one which I would recommend to anyone with an interest in autism and the sensory world.

Dr Luke Beardon

ACKNOWLEDGEMENTS

I would like to acknowledge and thank a number of people who played a role in supporting this book to fruition. To Natalie, Suzanne and Emma and previously Sarah from Jessica Kingsley for their patience and support. Thanks to Emily who originally showed faith in my ideas. A particular thank you to my brother in arms Dave who has been a great friend and a great sounding board throughout this project and throughout most of my life. Thanks also to Kerry for fulfilling a similar role closer to home. Thanks to Graham for the many helpful chats and to Darragh for his very practical help. My thanks to the Cronin family for their support.

Thanks to Luke for agreeing to be part of this project and also for offering insightful suggestions. I owe a debt of gratitude to Kirsten for being a constant source of support and for spurring me on when my energy flagged.

A particular thanks to the Heffernan family especially Sean and Kit, and thank you Kit for instilling my love of reading.

This book would not have been written without the contributions of a number of people that provided interviews which were integral to the book and were also a source of inspiration for wanting to write in the first instance. The humour, patience and honesty shown by all made the writing process all the easier and more enjoyable.

To Siobhan who has stood in solidarity with me and in support of all my endeavours, I am eternally grateful.

GLOSSARY

AS – Autism Spectrum

ASC – Autism Spectrum Condition

ASD – Autism Spectrum Disorder

Neurotypical – Person who is not on the Autism Spectrum

OT – Occupational Therapy

Introduction

Autism in a contemporary context

Television shows, movies, researchers, medical practitioners and writers have increasingly shown an interest in autism. As time goes by people with autism have also begun to publicly articulate their perspective and their experiences, as well as beginning to create a diverse autistic culture. This is to be hugely welcomed in light of the difficult history of autism in modern times. For the many people with autism who were misunderstood, misdiagnosed and often mistreated, the knowledge that there is now greater awareness of autism than ever should bring hope and optimism as to the future. A very significant step on the path to understanding the autistic perspective has been the burgeoning recognition of the part that sensory issues play in the lives of people with autism.

The benefits of support and Occupational Therapy assessment

It is imperative to acknowledge from the beginning that this book is not written to replace or undermine the work done by Occupational Therapists. It is my sincere hope that any Occupational Therapists that read the book will gain some ideas from it that will be useful to their work with clients with ASD (Autism Spectrum Disorder). It is also very important for me to state from the outset that I believe the work of Occupational Therapists will become ever more important to people with ASD, especially in terms of sensory difficulties. To this end I would strongly urge readers with ASD or parents/partners to seek Occupational Therapy assessments for themselves or their children or partners. Having acknowledged the importance of Occupational Therapists it is also important to note that not everyone will be able to access Occupational Therapy. This may be due to financial, geographical, logistical or personal reasons. For the huge cohort of people who fall into this category as well as those who have already had an assessment but need more support, my hope is that this book will provide some understanding and strategies that will be useful in everyday life. I have endeavoured to make the book as practical as possible while avoiding slavishly following any one particular intervention. Given the debate that surrounds every intervention that exists to support people with autism, I feel that it is wiser to take the parts that are useful from different interventions/therapies to create a suite of strategies that can be tailored to meet individual needs. I do not come from the school of thought that suggests that individual interventions are the only intervention that works for people with autism as to do so would imply, in my opinion, a lack of acknowledgement of the diversity and individuality of the autism community. I have stayed open minded about different interventions and hence my inclusion of the parts that I feel may be useful from different ones.

The significance of language and the writing style

'Language has sometimes been described as a "mirror of mind", so that the study of language should then give unique insight into human thought' (Chomsky 1996, p.1). Words are a potentially ambiguous and divisive means by which we convey messages, information and meaning. This has a particular resonance for people with autism where certain words have often been used in a way which we would consider to be derogatory (this is the case in contemporary times with pejorative use of the phrase 'autistic' because of certain behaviours that are deemed to not fit in with the norm).

The evolution of the words and language around autism, combined with the very welcome representations of autism by people on the Autism Spectrum (AS), have meant that a multiplicity of words and a complex language has created a culture. This complexity of culture and its influence on meaning has meant that certain parts of the autistic community have rejected certain words and language associated with autism while others in the autism community will embrace the same words and language. This is something I am very conscious of in my professional and academic life and in terms of the writing of this book. In recognition of the varying perspectives on different words and the language used around autism I have tried to be as inclusive of these different words and language as possible, while being aware that some people will welcome some of the terms I have used and reject others. To illustrate my point, some friends with autism will describe themselves as autistic while others will reject this term outright and prefer the term neurodiverse. It is not my intention to offend anyone or be divisive through the terms I have used throughout; on the contrary I have purposely used different terms as a means of not excluding anyone. Therefore throughout the text I will reference 'people with autism', 'people with Autism Spectrum Disorder' (ASD), 'people with Autism Spectrum Conditions' (ASC) or 'people on the Autism Spectrum' (AS). (At this point it is only fair for me to acknowledge that I have my own difficulties with some of these terms but it is not for me to force my own bias onto readers of this book.) These terms will be used interchangeably throughout as a way of recognising the diversity of preference amongst the autism community.

Similarly I have tried to strike the right tone in terms of addressing some of the issues covered in this book. This means that there are certain sections that speak directly to people on the Autism Spectrum, while in other sections I speak to parents of children with ASD as well as partners and spouses. I have also tried to represent the complexity of sensory issues as best I can throughout. This is not an easy task for two main reasons: first because sensory issues are a component part of what makes up the experiences of each individual, they are not prescriptive, and second because sensory issues are not necessarily always negative; for many people with autism their sensory differences can be positive and negative – sometimes simultaneously. I have endeavoured to represent both the positive and negative sides of sensory differences in Chapter 2 and Chapter 7 in particular. I have ensured some balance on the issue in recognition of the individualised nature of sensory experiences but I have also remained acutely aware of the profound difficulties that sensory issues can create in people's everyday lives. To this end while I have acknowledged the positives as much as possible, I have focused more on the difficulties created by sensory difficulties and explored practical ways of dealing with these difficulties. I have also used the terms 'sensory difference', 'sensory issues' and 'sensory difficulties' interchangeably throughout to reflect the variety of ways in which people with autism may experience their senses. This can obviously be relatively complex in the sense that, for example, any individual on the AS may have different sensory experiences through the same sensory systems at different times. It is my intention to reflect that complexity of experience through the use of these different terms in this book.

I have written the book in a style that I feel will be accessible to as many readers as possible. I have kept the language as straightforward as possible and presented the strategies in an easy to understand linear style.

The book is divided into two parts. The first part of the book, comprising the first and second chapter, discusses more theoretical and scientific concepts, as to leave these out would be to deny the reader access to how the senses work in the first instance as well as exploring the ways in which the senses work for people with ASD. The second part of the book, comprising Chapters 3 to 8, is more practical and strategy based while also drawing on the experiences of people with autism through a series of interviews.

The book is written primarily about sensory differences for people with ASD and different strategies that may be employed to manage those differences. It is, however, impossible in my opinion to write a book about sensory issues for people with autism without also addressing other connecting parts of what makes up a person. Therefore I address the connections between autism, memory and emotion in the book – specifically in Chapter 3 – but I also address the part that anxiety plays in the lives of people with autism and the connection between the experience of sensory differences and anxiety. Sensory issues in my opinion are intrinsically linked with anxiety and this comes up throughout the book. Similarly there are certain sections of the book that offer suggestions that are not inherently linked to sensory issues but which are imperative to cover in terms of the overall wellbeing of the readers of the book. An example of this is the section on Safety in Chapter 7.

Over time and through my work and research, it has become increasingly clear to me that sensory issues play a very significant role in the experience of autism for those on the AS. The clinical acknowledgement of this through the DSM-5 (Diagnostic and Statistical Manual of Mental Disorders) is to be welcomed but there is still a distance to be travelled before the full effects of sensory issues in autism are understood and supports are put in place to improve the daily lives of people who do experience sensory difficulties. Much of what I have written here is based on research, experience and perhaps most importantly the experiences of people with ASD that I have worked with over the years. It is impossible for me to cover every possible sensory experience for every person with autism as these experiences are individual to each person; however, my intention is that the experiences drawn on and the quotes used in this book will provide insight, understanding and support to as many people as possible.

Autism – difference or disability?

The construction of mainstream spaces and of society generally is predicated on agreed social 'norms'. These social 'norms' are culturally created and reproduced and serve to uphold the structures of society as a status quo. Those who exist outside of these 'norms' are often excluded and stigmatised, in a way that exposes societal fear of the 'other'. This 'other' may be manifest in, for example, different race, gender, sexuality or behaviour, from the 'norm'. Those with ASD are often 'othered' from the 'norm' due to the manifestations of autism that set them apart from mainstream society. The difficulties that people on the AS experience have been conceptualised as a deficiency in their ability to function 'normally', and ASD is therefore often categorised as a disability.

Following on from the work of Frith (1989) and Baron-Cohen (2000), amongst others, I view ASD not as a deficiency but rather as a difference. I view the concept of 'disability' in terms of autism as only being useful in so far as it allows access to services and payments which may only be accessed currently if the person is legally deemed 'disabled'. This legal definition does not take into account the spectrum of difference in human experience and ability, nor the potentially disabling nature of societal structures.

The supposed lack of 'normal sociability or communication is seen as a sign of disability' (Baron-Cohen 2000, p.4). However, this supposed lack of ability may also be viewed as a difference rather than deficiency. The ability to manage different sensory environments, interact or communicate socially exists on a spectrum, as with many supposed 'normal' abilities. The definition of what is normal and what is deficient may be seen as subjective, arbitrary and ambiguous. For example, how many people who do not have ASD struggle at some stage or other with a social situation, particularly one that is new to them or contains people who are not familiar? Social and communication abilities, as well as the ability to manage different sensory experiences, may vary depending on factors including the environment and the emotional state of the person in a given situation. The experiences of Temple Grandin (2006) who has ASD throws further light on this topic. Though an extremely capable and successful person by any objective standard (she is an engineer/designer, holder of a PhD, author, campaigner, and subject of a major television series), she describes her difficulties in trying to understand social expectations as being akin to trying to understand a different language.

The significance of the DSM-5

Though it has long been written about and discussed from the pioneers such as Ayers (1972) and DUNN (1999) to modern writers such as Bogdashina (2003), it has taken until the publication of the DSM-5 in 2013 to diagnostically recognise the significance of sensory issues for people on the AS. (We will discuss the diagnostic criteria in terms of sensory issues for people with autism in the DSM-5 in more detail in Chapter 2.) This does not mean that all is now settled and that people with ASD and sensory issues will have full understanding of the sensory differences they may experience. In fact in many ways this is the start of the process of acknowledging the part that sensory difficulties play and exploring ways of managing these difficulties.

It is my hope that this book will add in some small way to the evolving understanding of autism and the ways in which people with autism can manage their sensory environments, how flexibility of environment can be helpful and how a greater societal understanding is imperative to the creation of a pluralist sensory culture.

Chapter summaries

Chapter 1: The Sensory Systems

Chapter 1 begins by exploring what the senses are and how our experience of our senses may be influenced by context and environment. It also looks at synaesthesia, the crossing of senses where people may hear colours, for example. Central to this chapter will be an introduction to the ways in which the different sensory systems work, how the senses are integrated together and how this is essential to our ability to manage our environments. The senses are influenced by our memories and emotions and this chapter will also introduce the concept of the sense–memory–emotion paradigm which looks at the link between all three. The last section of the chapter will look specifically at the part memory and emotion plays in the experience of the senses.

Chapter 2: Sensory Differences in ASD

Chapter 2 builds on the areas covered in Chapter 1 and looks specifically at how the sensory systems work differently for many people with ASD. It looks especially at how the DSM-5 has acknowledged the importance of sensory issues for people with ASD and the ways in which it is presented and understood clinically. This involves looking at hypo- and hyper-sensitivity and how these different sensitivities influence the overall sensory profile of people with autism. The chapter finishes by discussing the potential positive as well as negative impacts of sensory differences, how these sensory differences can specifically be an advantage in certain circumstances, how synaesthesia seems to be connected to autism and the potential advantages of having synaesthetic abilities.

Chapter 3: The Sense–Memory– Emotion Paradigm

This chapter explores the specific ways in which memories and emotion play a part in how senses are perceived. It will look particularly at how people with ASD may be affected by the memories of certain spaces. It argues that clinically the difficulties people with ASD experience in certain spaces are attributed only to sensory issues as opposed to taking into account the memories or emotions that may create more difficulties than sensory issues would. This chapter argues for a recognition of the understandable human reactions that people with autism may experience in certain spaces.

The chapter finishes with a strategy as to how to manage the emotional resonances that may exist in certain spaces.

Chapter 4: School and College Spaces

Chapter 4 begins with an exploration of the school environment and how people with ASD may experience it. It then moves on to look at the specific difficulties that people with ASD may experience and why, before beginning to look at how a better sensory architecture may be created for the school. The next section of this chapter looks at college and the specific needs that may have to be met for people with ASD in college. The chapter ends by introducing the concept of the Learning Plan, which is a specific, person-centred individualised plan created for students with ASD – both in school and college – to afford them the best opportunities and provide the best supports to meet their learning and sensory needs.

Chapter 5: The Sensory Implications of Public Spaces, Social Spaces and Work Spaces

Chapter 5 looks at the different spaces and environments people with autism may experience sensory difficulties in, including pubs, nightclubs, supermarkets, streets, travel and work spaces. It will then look at creating sensory strategies that provide practical guidelines as to how people with sensory differences may manage the spaces that are problematic for them.

Chapter 6: Private Spaces and the Home

Having looked at the different social, public, school, college and work spaces that may contain sensory difficulties for people with autism, this chapter will explore the home as a private space that may be sensorily problematic. The chapter will begin by looking at the shared spaces of the home for couples with ASD and sensory issues or where one or other partner has ASD and sensory issues. The second part of this chapter will look at the shared home space from the perspective of parents of children with ASD and sensory differences.

Chapter 7: Intimacy and the Senses

This chapter examines the sensory implications of various aspects of intimacy or potential intimacy beginning with dating and online dating, including a discussion on the importance of safety in terms of dating generally. The next section of this chapter discusses the part sensory differences may play in intimacy and sex from both potentially positive and negative points of view. The last section of the chapter looks at the part sensory differences may play in relationships in general including the potential sensory implications of having children.

Chapter 8: Cyber Space

Having looked at both private and public spaces in previous chapters this last chapter explores cyber space and its sensory implications for people with autism. It begins with a discussion on the potential for cyber space to create new avenues of interaction. The potential negative and positive sensory implications of cyber space form a central part of the chapter which finishes by proposing a happy medium in terms of how cyber space may be used positively in the lives of people with sensory differences, and how sensory capital can be amassed as a way of managing difficult sensory spaces.

CHAPTER 1

The Sensory Systems

Environment and context

Wherever you currently are (while reading this book), sit down and take stock of your surroundings. Begin by looking at what is around you, and then listen to what sounds you may hear. As you are sitting, take note of your heartbeat and breathing. Are there any smells that you can detect? Or is there a lingering taste in your mouth? When taking in your surroundings, do any of the sights, sounds, smells or tastes remind you of anything? If so, how does that memory make you feel? This exercise is a simple way of beginning to become more aware of the array of sensory systems that work together in our bodies at any given time.[1] It is also a way of beginning to explore the relationship between our senses, our memories and our emotions (the sense–memory–emotion paradigm) that will feature in Chapter 3 of this book.

The interaction between human beings and our environment is mediated through our sensory systems.[2]

---

1   This touches on the philosophical concept of sense data, where we only perceive images of an object. In Hume's famous example, a table remains the same when we move closer or further away from it; the image we perceive of it changes depending on our perspective/distance.

2   Also known as modalities.

The sensory systems (through a complex series of pathways and connections throughout the body) help us regulate, decipher and negotiate our way through our particular environments. A useful definition of environment is the physical and social factors that surround us (Tomchek and Case-Smith 2009). Our physical environment is any space that we are in at any given time. For example, if we were sitting on a chair, at a desk, writing on a computer, this would be our current physical environment. In this situation our sensory systems would be working with each other to allow us to function in this environment. The social factors that are an intrinsic part of our environment can include people, with whom we interact at a given time or place.

Our physical environment changes when we share it with others. For instance, we may experience a street very differently when it is busy and full of people than when it is quiet and empty. More people on the street mean more sounds, less physical space, more chance of interaction. The inclusion of people in a space changes that space and in turn changes how we experience it sensorily.

Within the environment there are contexts, which are the personal, cultural and temporal (time) factors that exist within and around a person (AOTA 2011). Personal context means that we each experience our own worlds subjectively or individually as an accumulation of experiences, memories and emotions. Cultural context would include the religious, societal, geographical and country-specific factors that play a part in our lives. Temporal factors may also influence how we experience an environment. For example, we may find that a street is very busy at 9 p.m. on a Saturday night compared with the same street at 7 a.m. on a Monday morning. How busy a street is can affect how we experience the street sensorily and therefore temporal factors play an important part in the environment.

Sensory discrimination allows us to process the sensory inputs we receive in our different environments and contexts, and then create meaning from them. It enables us to decipher where and what something is (Miller *et al.* 2007). This constant processing and registration[3] that occurs through our sensory systems is taken for granted by most of us. We assume that different aspects of our lives exist as we experience them. For example, when most of us touch something we may assume that there is a universal way it feels because of its shape or material. However, our complex web of interconnected sensory systems work together to create a sense of what that shape and material feel like and mean to us individually. An example of this may be found in taste. Each of us have our own specific types of food that we enjoy that are unique to us. This is because our taste buds are different but it is also because our other senses influence whether we enjoy certain foods. What this means is that we may really enjoy eating chips because it brings back memories of a happy time in childhood, but we may not like or even eat potatoes generally! Therefore it is the unique combination of our own memories and taste that combine to create our enjoyment of the chips.

The synergy and interconnectedness between different sensory systems is manifest in synaesthesia[4] where a sensory experience associated with one modality stimulates another modality (Reber 1985). In essence, the senses 'cross over' one another in an unusual way. An example of synaesthesia would be having a particular auditory experience upon seeing a particular colour. In other words, some people 'hear colour'. Another example of this phenomenon is the experience of specific tastes when hearing or speaking certain words or numbers. There are many famous people with synaesthesia including jazz composer Duke Ellington, physicist

---

3   The detection of sensation (Kandel, Schwartz and Jessell 2000).
4   First described by Francis Galton in the nineteenth century.

Richard Feynman and painter David Hockney (Purves, Brannon *et al.* 2008). Synaesthesia is also relatively common amongst people with Autism Spectrum Disorders (Bogdashian 2003; Tammet 2006, 2009). These experiences of synaesthesia may seem odd, but most of us have experiences like this. For example, psychological research has demonstrated that most people experience the colour blue as being cold and the colour red as being warm (Reber 1985) and in fact interior designers use this phenomenon to their advantage to create certain experiences through the use of specific colours.

Our sensory systems are in a state of constant motion, processing, mediating and deconstructing the constant flow of information that we receive through internal and external sources in order for us to be able to function in our environment and contexts. It may be best to think of the sensory system as being akin to a filter, which takes in masses of information every second through all our senses and processes the information to be deemed either 'necessary' or 'unnecessary'. This allows the information deemed as 'necessary' to become part of our cognition.[5]

The earlier part of this chapter introduced the sense–memory–emotion paradigm. Consider this: if we are anxious or stressed we may experience our sensory world differently than if we are relaxed and calm. An example of this for people with ASC who have sensory difficulties is a busy supermarket. At its busiest, the variety and intensity of sensory inputs in the supermarket may make people with an ASC feel anxious or stressed. Conversely, in that same supermarket at one of its quietest times, people with an ASC may feel relatively calm and relaxed. This illustrates how we can have two very different experiences of the exact same space. This is directly as a result of the information processed by our sensory systems. Therefore, as our sensory systems are linked to our memories,

---

5   The process of obtaining knowledge through our senses.

our memories may dictate how we feel about going to the supermarket. If the busy supermarket is an overwhelming sensory experience for someone with an ASC, the next time they go there they may still remember what the supermarket was like before and how this made them feel. This in turn may influence their desire and ability to cope with the supermarket when they return. This may happen in any other space that may contain potential sensory difficulties.

The sensory systems (the relatively brief science part of the chapter!)

The sensory systems work as part of the nervous system. The nervous system is made up of a series of cells and nerves which carry messages around the body. It is comprised of two types of cells: neurons, which are specialised cells designed to transmit information in the form of electrical or chemical signals and are the basis for sensation, behaviour and cognitive abilities; and neuroglial cells, which hold nervous tissue together.[6]

The nervous system is also divided into two main parts: the central nervous system and the peripheral nervous system. The central nervous system consists of the brain and the spinal cord while the peripheral nervous system consists of the *somatic* nervous system and the *autonomic* nervous system. The *somatic* nervous system consists of peripheral nerve fibres which carry messages to and from the peripheral organs of the body such as the limbs. For example, if we touch something hot the message is transmitted through the fingers via the central nervous system and into the brain. The *autonomic* nervous system consists of the inner organs and involves the cells and nerves which carry out unconscious functioning

6   Glia coming from the Greek for glue.

such as digestion, breathing and heartbeat (Purves, Brannon, *et al.* 2008).

Neurons

Neurons are made up of dendrites, which are tentacle-like limbs that receive information from other neurons, and axons, which transmit information to other neurons. This information travels through the connections between cells known as synapses using electrical based neurotransmitters.[7] The sensory systems are based on specific sensory receptor cells which carry information through to neurons in the sensory systems.[8] This causes them to create an electrical current which in turn fires an action potential[9] which carries the current from neuron to neuron and eventually to processing centres in the central nervous system. The processing centres then send these messages to the brain. Processing of sensory information is flexible, therefore at various processing stations a variety of stimuli are detected but the stations react to the most prescient in a given situation. For instance, if we are in a room where someone has a radio on with music playing very loudly but we accidentally touch a hot stove, our senses will adapt to the different stimuli and recoil our hand from the stove as a matter of precedence.[10] Therefore the detection of sensory stimuli allows us to negotiate through and with our environment, in terms of physical and behavioural responses.

---

7   Neurotransmitters are any substance that serve to carry communication/information across the gap between neurons; examples include dopamine and serotonin.

8   Known as afferent neurons.

9   Action potentials are the electrical changes that happen in a cell when it is fired by signals/messages.

10 Though this is not always the case as we will discover in Chapter 2.

It is thought that the key to understanding how neural messaging works is to examine the starting point of the signal. For example, if the starting point is in the eye this determines how and where the information will be conveyed and what action may follow from that. However, it is still unclear exactly how the neurons generate perception, perception being the processing of sensory data into meaning (Hock 2013).

Sensory perception[11]

Sensory perception begins in rudimentary form in infancy as infants try to make sense of their world. Much of this perception in infants is generated only by sight and infants are still very much reliant on adults to help them to function in their environment (Fantz 1961). However there are a number of sensory modalities which are used by humans to interpret their environment. These are focused around the five senses[12] of sight, sound, taste, smell and touch but also include the vestibular and proprioceptive systems.[13]

Sight

Sight or vision is a fundamental aspect of human sensory interpretation. It allows us to judge distances and assess the size, shape and colour of something. Vision can be thought of as having two systems – movement (where) and form (what) (Schneider 1969), though both work simultaneously.

---

11 In Ayurvedic philosophy the senses are all attached to elements, i.e. Ether for hearing, Air for touch, Fire for vision, Water for taste, Earth for smell.

12 There are different views as to how many senses there are, generally varying from five to eleven different senses.

13 See below for a detailed description of the vestibular and proprioceptive systems.

Sight activates approximately half of the brain and so is one of the most important of the senses. Sight works much like a camera. Light passes through the surface of the eye (the cornea), and the cornea then focuses that light on to the retina which consists of two types of receptors: rods and cones. Rods respond to less light while cones respond to more light.[14] The visual information gathered in the retina is transferred via an action potential to cells[15] which gather together into the optic nerve and are passed much like a cable car to the brain. These cable cars split and send information from the left of the visual field to the right hemisphere of the brain and vice versa. Sight is very important for cognition as it is the easiest way for us to make meaning or sense of our environment.[16] It is also important for communication; for example, if we were to buy a new dress and wanted to describe it to others, we might start with the colour, then the cut/shape/length, all of which are garnered from our vision (though not exclusively).

Sound

Hearing, or the auditory system, plays an important role in how we interpret our environment and how we interact with others. It not only detects general sounds and noises, but it recognises speech and is therefore instrumental in communication. Hearing works by recognising the displacement of air molecules which are caused by changes in air pressure. These changes in air pressure are called sound waves. The sound waves travel through the inner ear known as the cochlea. The cochlea contains the basilar membrane.

---

14 There are usually over one hundred million rods in the eye and roughly five to six million cones.

15 Known as ganglion cells.

16 Though people with visual impairments often cope very well without the benefit of this sense.

THE SENSORY SYSTEMS   31

This is a thin membrane covered in tiny hairs that are stimulated by sound waves. The basilar membrane works by transferring these sound waves into neural signals which are then sent to the brain. The auditory system generally has the ability to distinguish between noises and focus on one while 'turning down' another. For instance, if someone is talking to us while we are simultaneously listening to an interesting item on the radio we may be able to 'turn down' the sound of the person talking to us and tune in to the radio item.

Sound can also be connected with memory and emotion. As a demonstration of this, if we were to think of moments in our life when a song has reminded us of a particular place, time or person, this generates an emotional response of happiness, sadness or melancholia.

Taste

Taste[17] and smell[18] are very much linked as both are chemical-based sensory systems. Taste is dependent on the olfactory senses although sensory cells on the tongue also play a part. The human tongue has between 500 and 10,000 taste buds, each of which has approximately 50 receptor cells called microvilli which send messages to the sensory processing areas of the brain[19] (Gazzaniga and Heatherington 2006). For an easy experiment in how taste and smell are linked, we can just block our nose while eating something and note how the intensity of the taste is diminished by doing so.

---

17 Also known as gustation.
18 Also known as olfaction.
19 Messages are sent through the medulla, into the thalamus which ultimately sends them to the cortex area of the brain.

Smell

Smell works by sending nerve impulses to what is called the olfactory bulb. The olfactory bulb is the part of the brain that governs smell and it disseminates the information received to other parts of the brain.[20] The information is passed through the prefrontal cortex,[21] which decides on whether a smell is pleasant or not, while the amygdala processes the intensity of the smell. Smell works when airborne bacteria enter the nose and are detected by olfactory receptors (Gazzaniga and Heatherington 2006). Because the amygdala and prefrontal cortex of the brain are also implicated in memory and emotion, certain smells can also often be evocative for people of a particular time, place or person.

Touch

Touch, or the tactile system,[22] is a complex series of interactive receptors which include responses to intensity of touch, heat and pain. Discriminative touch is what we use to distinguish what it is we are touching. The receptors for discriminative touch are mainly based in the skin of the fingers, toes and face as opposed to the torso. There are separate cell receptors for heat and cold based on the surface of the skin though both can be stimulated simultaneously. Pain receptors warn the body of damage that may be occurring to it, though there are ways of mitigating against certain pain by, for example, manipulating the skin around a source of pain which stimulates other cell receptors and consequently overwhelms

---

20 For example to the amygdala which also governs memory and emotion. Taste, smell and emotion are all closely linked.

21 The prefrontal cortex governs the examination of thoughts and sensory information and decides on where to send the information or what action may flow from the information.

22 Also known as the haptic sense.

pain receptors (Melzack and Wall 1982). A simple example of this is if we were to bang our arm on something then rub around it and find that this action eases the pain. The tactile system also plays an important part in the texture of foods as we use it to feel the shape of the food in the mouth.

Proprioceptive system

Proprioception[23] is the awareness of the body in space. It comes from the nervous system but is not based on tactile cell receptors on the surface or skin of the body. It is based on proprioceptive cells which tell us where our body is without needing to orient ourselves through external factors such as touching something. This process involves signals being sent through receptors[24] including muscle spindles and tendons,[25] through the spinal cord and back to the brain so that we unconsciously understand where our arms and legs are at a given time without having to constantly visually check.[26] Proprioception is therefore about the ability to orient the limbs in a particular space and time in complex patterns (such as in sport) not normally associated with everyday activities. However, it is also about the ability to carry out everyday activities such as walking, washing the dishes or playing pool.

---

23 Meaning receptors for self, proprioception is also categorised as being the philosophical opposite of exteroception which informs us through our senses as to what is going on outside our bodies.

24 Known as mechanoreceptors.

25 The beautifully named Golgi tendons.

26 Though there is also conscious proprioception or kinaesthesia – literally meaning the sensation of motion.

Vestibular system

The vestibular system is related to our sense of balance, gravity and self-motion by orienting our head and thus our body in space. Receptors are spaced out in different parts of the inner ear canals to detect the different movements, directions and speed of the head. These different receptors are called accelerometers and angular velocity sensors. They send a continuous flow of information to sensory processing centres in the brainstem and cerebellum[27] (Purves *et al.* 2012). This in turn keeps us balanced when we are walking and also enables us to move our head up and down without losing balance. For example, it is our vestibular system that enables us to sit in a chair and write while looking from the computer keyboard up to the computer screen and back all without falling off our chair.

Sensory integration

Although different sensory systems have their own independent and individual receptor cells, they also must work in conjunction with each other in order to allow us to function as physical, sentient bodies with agency (autonomy) in a variety of environments. The collusion of the senses allows us to participate in our life world in ways that many of us never consciously consider. This includes the unconscious yet very dynamic flow of messages through cells and neurons that are being relayed constantly throughout the body. This means accepting and relaying a massive amount of information which, when processed, enables us to function in

---

27 Neurons travel through the brainstem which enables signals to be transferred between the brain and the spinal cord. The cerebellum contains neurons that carry messages between the muscles and the parts of the brain that enable motor function.

ways that we view as basic but which are extremely complex in their creation and execution. It may be useful to imagine the sensory systems as being like an orchestra where all the instruments are playing in harmony to create music, though if any instruments are out of tune, are listened to in isolation, or are not playing to the same tempo as the other instruments then it changes the music and disrupts its harmony.

There are many theories as to how the various senses work in concert with each other and this is termed 'binding'. For example, one theory suggests that there are specialised neurons whose function it is to bring together the various sensory perceptions from the sensory systems and combine them to create overall perception. There are problems with this theory however as there is no evidence from current understanding of the brain that such specialised neurons exist. It is thought to be more likely that there are a variety of neurons spread throughout the brain involved in this type of multi-sensory binding. It is also worth noting that there are new theories on brain development and function appearing at an extraordinarily rapid rate, and old theories about the brain being debunked almost as rapidly (see magazines such as *New Scientist* or any publications reporting neuroscientific research for discussion on the rapid pace of such developments).

Memory and the senses

All memories begin with the processing of information through the various sensory systems. Memory is then formed into a bank of information stored in our brain which allows us to learn, to communicate, to apply experience and to make sense of situations and emotions, and it influences us on a cognitive and behavioural level. In scientific terms memory is the process of creating indelible neural marks[28] in the brain which are thought to stem from changing synaptic connections between neurons. Memory is not a monolithic functioning process; it is divided into different subtypes, the most prescient being: working memory, long-term memory, declarative and non-declarative memory, and sensory memory. Working memory (short-term memory) is information that is only retained for a short period of time (usually a few seconds). For most people our short-term memory allows us to recall small segments of information for short periods. This would mean, for example, being able to recall seven to nine digits for usually no more than 20 seconds, unless we rehearse and learn the information. Long-term memory is memory that is 'permanent'. To use a computer analogy it is memory which is stored on a hard drive though it differs from a computer in that it is fallible and open to the various ravages of the human life course (time, experience, etc.). Information can be moved from short-term to long-term memory. For instance, it is theorised that in cases where the information may be useful in the longer term, such as information about the environment, this may be transferred from short-term memory to long-term memory. Another theory holds that consistently learning and rehearsing something over a period of time ingrains that information to the brain's hard drive.

Declarative memory is the memories which are stored in the consciousness and can actively be sought and expressed through language. Examples of declarative memory are phone numbers of family or friends, past events, or lines from a poem. Non-declarative memory is the 'unconscious' skills that we all use at various times of most days and include using a phone, driving, reciting a poem or using a computer keyboard to write words. Though all memories are derived initially from

---

28 Known as Engrams.

the sensory systems, sensory memory (the actual information as it is received in terms of smells, lights, etc.) impacts on the nervous system very briefly before disappearing. For example, if we look at a picture then look away we can conjure the image in our mind briefly before it fades. Sensory memory is subdivided into two very important categories: *echoic* and *iconic* memory. *Echoic* memory is auditory sensory memory and *iconic* is visual sensory memory. Many researchers believe that echoic and iconic sensory memory work in conjunction with each other to allow us to experience the sensory world in a continuous flow rather than in disparate or discreet individual sensations (Gazzaniga and Heatherington 2006).

Memories are currently understood to be stored in the cortex mainly but also throughout the brain.[29] The areas of the brain that memories are stored in are thought to be linked to the original area of processing, for example visual memories stored in the visual cortices of the brain.[30]

Memory is intrinsically linked to learning. It is the method by which we recall activities, information or experiences and apply what is stored in our memories to our present or new environments. Most of what we know of the world is not hardwired into our brains at birth but is learned and recalled over the course of our lives. We recall books we read, stories we were told, music we listened to and art we appreciated. The question of what is learned and what is intrinsic to us as humans has been a deep philosophical, existential and medical debate which has been ongoing since Socrates (and before). Memory therefore is not only a method of recall and learning; it is

---

29 Given that the brain is an organ there is much speculation as to the possibility of memory being stored or at least held in other organs in the body; for example, it has been reported that some organ donation recipients have reported memories which have later been attributed to the donor.

30 Cortices are an area that serve as a terminal point for incoming information from sensory cells.

essential to who we are as individuals, as what we remember plays a vital role in our sense of self, our very identity. Memory is also individual in terms of how subjective our memory of shared experiences can be. For instance, the subjective qualities of memory are often illustrated when recalling an event we may have attended with a friend in the past but when we begin to recall and discuss it with the friend, we both may have very different memories and perspectives on it.

Memory is intrinsic to who we are in the present moment and who we will evolve into. Each passing moment has memories attached to it, but we do not retain all of this information. The information that is retained becomes part of our learning and shapes who and what we become. This is an ever-evolving process that not only includes learning, subjective experiences and our identities, but is also temporally (time) dependent. The passage of time in conjunction with the human life course is, therefore, an extremely important factor, not only in terms of the physical, emotional and mental evolution of a person from birth through childhood, adolescence and old age, but also in terms of the effects time has on memory. The old adage 'time heals all' refers to the ability of the brain to filter out, or fade to sepia, unwanted or bad memories. This means that through the life course people often forget aspects of, or incidents in, their lives which bring negative emotions.[31] Memories, as described previously, carry emotions with them, and in fact it is the same area of the brain that governs memory and emotion.[32] Memory and emotions are therefore neurologically linked, and this transfers into the real-world experiences of people in everyday life as illustrated through the example above.

---

31 This does not always happen; some people carry bad memories or traumatic memories with them through their entire lives.

32 The hippocampus.

Sense and emotion

The history of emotions is one fraught with lack of understanding and ironically fear and contempt. In ancient Greek mythology, for example, many of the woes of humankind were attributed to emotions such as envy and jealousy while in Christian terms the Ten Commandments talk about the sins of lust, envy and greed (Editors of Time-Life 1994). Even in more contemporary times madness has often been negatively constructed as being caused or defined by out-of-control emotions.

The purpose of emotion is to assess the meaning and significance of cues in the environment (social and otherwise) and to then regulate behaviour accordingly by engaging multiple neural circuits across the brain. The processing of emotion through the brain is still an area under research by the scientific/medical community.[33] As previously mentioned, emotions are linked with memory and are processed in similar parts of the brain, and in fact we are more likely to remember things that had a strong emotional impact on us.

Emotions play an elemental part in all our lives. We feel joy at seeing our children being born or our team win the championship; we feel pride at our academic, professional or personal achievements; we feel relief when we get home after a long journey; we often feel stress and anxiety while on that journey; we feel sad when people we know die; we feel frightened when we watch a horror movie; we feel frustrated when we perceive politicians as dealing in rhetoric. Every significant

---

33 However, the limbic system is involved with controlling emotions and manages the autonomic nervous system (Mildner 2008). The limbic system is a series of structures that include the amygdala, the hippocampus and various parts of the cortex, including the prefrontal cortex (Siegel, Sapru and Siegel 2006). What is also known is that emotions do not follow linear patterns but rather work in complex processing loops which also means that emotional processing happens in an overlapping fashion (Coch, Fischer and Dawson 2007).

moment in our lives has an emotional resonance for us. This does not mean that the significant moments always create the same emotions in those experiencing them. For example, many people in very stressful or difficult jobs, such as soldiers or members of the police force, may use humour as a method of coping with very extreme circumstances, while others may feel fear or sorrow in the same circumstances. For some people everyday situations may cause anxiety, while for others they may induce joy. An example in literature may be found in Albert Camus' existential classic *The Outsider* (Camus 2000). In Camus' story the chief protagonist Meursault does not cry at his mother's funeral (despite the fact that he understands he is expected to cry) as he does not feel any sorrow that his mother has died.

In general, human beings are emotional creatures whose behaviour is dictated by emotional factors as much as it is by logic, and in fact 'logic' can be very heavily influenced by emotion. Every possible thought that we have brings with it an emotion, even if that emotion is not felt strongly or even registered consciously. Many of us become so conditioned to certain thoughts and behaviours that we don't consciously register the emotion that comes with it.[34] Many of us have also developed ways of suppressing emotions that are negative or painful for us. Often the suppression happens at the level of the memory that triggers the emotion. This means we suppress the memory and therefore suppress the emotion. For instance, we may have had one or more bad experiences at school. It is common for people to suppress the bad memories associated with school as these memories often cause a strong emotional response when recalled.

---

34 Most of us watch television and are having some emotional response to it, but we are not consciously aware of the emotion.

CHAPTER 2

Sensory Differences in ASD

It has become increasingly clear that sensory differences play a central role in the experience of autism for many people with ASD. Both scientific research (Dunn, Myles and Orr 2002) and first-hand accounts (Gerland 2003; Grandin 2006; Grandin and Scariano 1986; Williams 1999) have shown us that sensory issues manifest in numerous ways in the lives of people with ASD and these issues have consequences for their daily lives. There are also numerous studies and books providing statistics on the numbers of people with ASD who have sensory differences, with for example Mayes and Calhoun in 1999 reporting that 100 per cent of the participants in their study showed sensory difficulties across the various sensory categories. While there is a large degree of variance across other studies it is clear that sensory issues are a feature in the lives of a significant proportion of people with autism and increasing empirical evidence shows us that this is the case (e.g. Baranek 2002; Ben-Sasson *et al.* 2009; Crane, Goddard and Pring 2009).

Sensory issues, therefore, play an important part in how people with autism experience their world. Much of what has been written about sensory differences in autism has tended to focus on how these differences are somehow aberrant or do not fit in with the 'norm'. As stated previously, sensory issues may create difficulties for people with ASD; however, sensory difficulties may also be advantageous or pleasurable in certain circumstances. Therefore the seven senses may be affected (positively or negatively, sometimes both) by sensory differences.

Hyper- and hypo-sensitivity

As mentioned in the Introduction, the latest Diagnostic Statistical Manual, under Autism Spectrum Disorder 299.00 (F84.0), has included sensory issues as part of the diagnostic criteria in ASD for the first time. The DSM divides sensory issues into *hypo-sensitivity* and *hyper-sensitivity* (we will discuss both in more detail presently):

> Hyper- or hyporeactivity to sensory input or unusual interests in sensory aspects of the environment (e.g., apparent indifference to pain/temperature, adverse response to specific sounds or textures, excessive smelling or touching of objects, visual fascination with lights or movement). (American Psychiatric Association 2013)

One could reasonably argue that while other aspects of the DSM–5 diagnostic criteria are not specified as being as a result of sensory issues, in fact sensory issues may play a part, for example:

> Stereotyped or repetitive motor movements, use of objects, or speech (e.g., simple motor stereotypies, lining up toys or flipping objects, echolalia, idiosyncratic phrases). (American Psychiatric Association 2013)

This may include self-stimulation (stimming) for people seeking sensory inputs.

> Insistence on sameness, inflexible adherence to routines, or ritualized patterns or verbal nonverbal behaviour (e.g., extreme distress at small changes, difficulties with transitions, rigid thinking patterns, greeting rituals, need to take same route or eat food every day). (American Psychiatric Association 2013)

The above may include eating the same food every day as it does not cause the potential sensory difficulties that new or different foods may. Sticking to particular routines in terms of place or space may also be as a result of sensory difficulties in spaces that may contain noises, smells or other sensory inputs that many people with autism may find distressing.

Hyper-sensitivity is a response to sensory stimuli that is greater than what may be expected considering what the sensory stimuli are, and in comparison with people who do not have sensory difficulties. This response may often generate the fight or flight[1] response (particularly in spaces that may contain an overwhelming array of sensory inputs) and is also termed sensory defensiveness (Kuhanek and Watling 2010).

Hypo-sensitivity is a response to sensory stimulation that is less than what may be expected considering what the sensory stimuli are, and in comparison with people who do not have sensory difficulties. This may mean, for example, that the individual may appear indifferent to the pain of a broken bone or extreme temperatures.

Sensory seeking

The third domain of sensory differences in ASD is sensory-seeking behaviours. This manifests in the person seeking out sensory stimulation through any of the senses. Though many researchers identify sensory-seeking behaviour as a distinct

---

1   Also known as the autonomic nervous system response.

third domain of sensory difference (Baranek *et al.* 2006; Lane *et al.* 2011; Rogers and Ozonoff 2005), other researchers in the field categorise sensory-seeking behaviours as being part of hypo-sensitivity (Dunn 2007).

People with sensory difficulties may have a mixed sensory profile in that they may have features of both hypo-sensitivity (including sensory-seeking behaviour) as well as hyper-sensitivity. An example of this may be seen in touch where someone may have hypo-sensitivity and appear indifferent to pain as mentioned before, but may be hyper-sensitive to light touch such as someone brushing against them which they may experience as being deeply uncomfortable or painful. The experience, therefore, of sensory differences is an individual one to each person. The sensory differences each individual experiences may also be influenced by many of the factors that play a part in shaping every human being such as schooling, parenting, sibling relationships, friendships, isolation, socio-economic and geographical factors amongst others.[2]

Diverse sensory experiences

Though sensory differences are categorised into hypo- or hyper-sensitivity in the DSM–5, there are numerous manifestations of sensory differences for people with ASD. Not all sensory differences are necessarily negative, as mentioned previously. There are many examples of adaptive sensory behaviour[3] or

---

2   Autism is described in psychological terms as a disjunctive category in that no two people with autism are the same.

3   So-called maladaptive behaviour may often be adaptive, i.e. different sensory behaviours may often serve a positive purpose (Reisman and Hanschu 1992).

of sensory differences which may have positive as well as negative impacts on people's lives. These sensory differences revolve around the seven senses of: auditory, visual, olfactory, gustatory, tactile, vestibular and proprioceptive differences. However, sensory differences may also become manifest in experiences such as synaesthesia.

Auditory

Auditory differences are common for people with ASD. These differences may manifest as hearing some sounds more loudly than others[4] or hearing 'background' noise rather than more centralised noise – for example, not being able to hear a person talking in a café where there are other extraneous noises such as others talking or music[5] – or it may mean only being able to sense sound in one ear. There are many theories that abound in terms of the reasons for auditory differences for people with ASD including overconnectivity of short-distance neurons and underconnectivity of long-distance neurons (Courchesne and Pierce 2005a, 2005b). Occelli *et al.* (2013) amongst others have speculated that people with ASD over-focus on specific sensory inputs leading to a lack of integration of different sensory inputs, or the processing of each sensory input independently – to the detriment of other simultaneous sensory inputs. This is seen as also being congruent with the concept of weak central coherence (not being able to see the wider context, focusing on minutiae). Many people with ASD may also have difficulties integrating visual information with auditory (De Pape, Hall and Tillman 2012), for example matching the movement of a person's mouth with the noise

---

4 Also known as hyperacusis.
5 In general, people with autism appear to have differences in how sounds are processed and segregated.

words) they are making. In practice, what this means is that many people with ASD experience sounds differently and this can have ramifications for everyday life.[6] It has been speculated that difficulties with auditory/visual processing may also cause social developmental difficulties for people with ASD, for instance, not fully developing the ability to recognise parental speech may create social/language difficulties. It is also common for people with ASD who have auditory differences to be unresponsive to their own name being spoken.[7]

It is not to say, however, that all sounds are unwelcome or that the areas of auditory difference described thus far are necessarily negative. Having the ability to focus intently on particular sounds can be extremely useful for musicians, sound engineers, technicians, music producers, mechanics, engineers, doctors or surgeons or possibly even spies! This 'inability' to integrate sounds may also therefore be a very useful ability in many cases. Many people with autism find certain sounds more pleasurable than neurotypicals may. Some people with autism who seek auditory stimulation may really enjoy noisy spaces – much more so than most neurotypicals. The ability to 'tune out' certain sounds may be useful in many contexts: it may help concentration on certain tasks and it may improve the person's ability to perform tasks in areas that others may find too noisy. Other people with autism may be able to revel in the nuance of music through the appreciation of 'hidden' notes or rhythms that most neurotypicals may find difficult to hear.

---

6   The ability to integrate these senses is tested using the McGurk effect which measures participant response to incongruous visual/auditory stimuli.

7   Which can often create tensions with the person's parent/partner/ sibling who may feel that the person is being rude or defiant.

Vision

Differences in visual perception are relatively common for people with ASD. It is speculated that these differences may be because of different sensory functioning in the visual cortex of people with autism and, similarly to auditory difference, is often connected to an inability to integrate different sensory stimuli when they co-occur. What this may mean is that some people with autism may tend to have difficulty focusing on the local while the peripheral appears more clear. This may manifest in an inability to recognise a person's face (also called prosopagnosia – literally face blindness). Donna Williams (1999) gives an example of this where she will meet people in front of whatever building she is due to meet them in, as this places the emphasis on the other person to recognise and approach her (this is the case even with friends). It may also mean the opposite – an ability to focus on the local while finding it very difficult to visually contextualise. Alternatively, or concurrently, it may also create difficulties with depth perception or distance. This may lead to apparent 'clumsiness' or difficulties with occupations requiring dexterity, or difficulties with sports.

However, these visual differences may also create pleasurable experiences or be very useful in terms of hobbies/interests or occupations. For instance, the ability to focus in on particular sights may be very pleasurable or even hypnotic for some people with ASD who have reported the pleasure (apart from any sentimental feelings) they may derive from looking at Christmas lights or other objects that are localised in a wider visual context, or objects that have a visual rhythm – such as any form of flashing lights. Having the ability to focus in on minute or localised objects may be very useful to people who do dexterous and/or physical work, or work that may involve seeking out visual minutiae including doctors, surgeons, musicians, scientists, researchers, soldiers, police or government officials.

Olfactory

There is relatively little research on the specific olfactory sensory differences people with ASD may experience. Much research around sensory differences is generalised and tends to take a broader approach which includes all sensory differences, or differences in sensory perception. There has been some specific research however with Suzuki's study/research (Suzuki *et al.* 2003) showing differences in the ability of people with autism in his cohort to identify certain odours, Benetto's study (Benetto, Kuschner and Hyman 2007) showed differences in his cohort of 10–18 year olds and Schoen *et al.* in 2009 who showed olfactory differences in over half their cohort, though Tavassoli and Baron-Cohen's 2011 research (Tavassoli 2012) found no significant difference in olfactory ability in their ASD cohort as compared to a neurotypical control group. What is significant in terms of the research around the olfactory differences and sensory differences generally is the contrasting results between self-report questionnaires and lab-based research. In general it has been found that self-report questionnaires tend to show much higher rates of sensory difficulties generally than lab-based research. Tavassoli and Baron-Cohen (2011) surmise that it may be anxiety or stress that influence sensory experiences and if these anxieties or stresses are related to environment then it may explain the variance between the self-report questionnaires and lab-based research. As with other senses, it is also speculated that a difficulty in processing discrete sensory inputs may lead to an overwhelming amount of information being received which may in turn affect processing.[8]

On a day-to-day basis, olfactory differences may have some profound effects, both negative and positive.

---

8   It is also speculated that impairments in y-aminobutyric acid also known as GABA (a neurotransmitter that serves as an inhibitor of sensory input) may create enhanced sensitivity.

For example, being overly sensitive to smell could mean not using aftershave, soap, deodorant or perfume. This in turn may lead to poor hygiene which may create difficulties in social contexts. Olfactory issues may manifest in interpersonal relationships, if the other person is wearing perfume for example that may be overwhelming. It may cause people with olfactory sensitivity to avoid changing rooms in gyms, or for sports, both of which may have social or health consequences. On the other hand, lack of a defined sense of smell may also create the same issues if the person does not smell what others may find 'offensive', as then they may not prioritise washing themselves or their clothes.

Sense of smell is also intrinsically linked with memory as we explored in the first chapter. Therefore certain smells may be evocative of a particular time or space which could have negative connotations. For example, the smell of bleached floors may be evocative of school for many people with ASD and given that 90–95 per cent of people with ASD have been bullied (Tantam 2009) it is likely that this evocation may be problematic.

However, on the positive side, having an acute sense of smell may be pleasurable when smelling certain odours. This may mean being able to derive huge pleasure from everyday odours that others may barely register. It may also mean being able to detect or differentiate between odours in a way that most others would be incapable of. This may be useful in certain occupations such as working in scientific laboratories, perfumeries or wine tasters.

Having a less acute sense of smell may also be useful in terms of not being bothered by odours that others may find offensive/overwhelming. This may be useful in certain occupations where strong smells are involved such as factory work, refuse, hygiene or sanitation.

Gustatory

Gustatory sensory differences may create many difficulties in the eating of certain foods (Grandin 1996) with 'problem' eating behaviours reported in up to 75 per cent of children with ASD (Cemak, Curtin and Bandini 2010; Nadon *et al.* 2011). This may involve sensitivity to certain textures, tastes or smells. These gustatory differences for people with ASD have generally been under-researched with Benetto (2007) and Tavassoli and Baron-Cohen (2011) being among the few studies that have taken place. Similarly to other sensory differences for people with ASD, it is not known for certain what causes these differences but given the link between taste and smell, it may be safe to speculate that the reasons explored in the olfactory section earlier are most likely applicable to gustatory also. It has been speculated however that differences in the thalamus (which is involved in the processing of taste) of people with autism compared with neurotypicals may contribute to different gustatory experiences.

Gustatory differences include taste and smell (which as we explored in Chapter 1 are intrinsically linked). However, many people with autism also experience gustatory sensitivities in texture. This may manifest in difficulties eating certain shaped foods or foods with a certain texture. In many cases people with autism have a specific diet that revolves around foods that they can tolerate. Often times this means simple foods, such as pasta or potatoes, without sauces or other condiments which would change the texture of the food. The National Autistic Society[9] has suggested that other gustatory differences may involve eating anything from mud to grass (this is more likely to be in children with autism but not exclusively) which may provide pleasant textures. On the opposite side of this many people with autism will seek out

---

9   www.autism.org.uk

particularly spicy foods and may appear impervious to the hot sensation this may create in the mouth. In general the disadvantage of a restricted diet due to sensory difficulties may lead to health problems, particularly if the diet excludes fruit, vegetables, seeds, etc. It may also have financial implications if, for example, the only foods tolerated are specialised and therefore expensive. There may also be social implications of a restricted diet meaning that eating in restaurants or cafés might be very difficult due to lack of availability of preferred foods or lack of flexibility on the part of eating establishments to accommodate certain food preferences.

The advantages of gustatory differences are that it may mean being able to tolerate very hot foods as stated above and this can have dietary/health benefits. For example, chillies are involved in the release of endorphins.[10] It also means that people who have gustatory hypo-sensitivity may be able to tolerate a variety of different foods which may be new to the palate; this may be useful in travel, for example. It may be useful in the catering, hospitality or restaurant business. It may also mean only being able to tolerate foods of a certain type which happen to be very healthy such as fruit or vegetables. In this instance it may mean having an extremely healthy diet.

Tactile

Touch serves a primary, fundamental function in human development as well as in the development of other species. It serves to create social connections, it establishes relationships and is thought to have an evolutionary role in terms of co-operation and establishing dominance. For instance, body language experts will often refer to how certain methods of

---

10 The active 'hot' ingredient in the chilli activates pain receptors which in turn trigger the release of endorphins.

shaking hands – say, with one hand on the other person's elbow – show dominance. Watching how others touch is also instructive in our development as it teaches us how to use touch as part of communication. From a kiss to a kick, from a caress to a punch, ultimately the primary function of touch is as a tool for communication. It is a part of building relationships with parents and loved ones as well being a means for defence against attack. It is therefore related to our emotions in that a caress may give us pleasure, make us feel safe, wanted or loved, while a blow may make us feel fearful, unwanted/unloved, isolated or angry. How we receive or deliver touch is inextricably linked with our feelings.

It is estimated that approximately 70 per cent of people with ASD experience tactile sensory differences (Baranek *et al.* 2006). Amongst the sensory differences that people with ASD may experience, it could be argued that this has the most direct influence on people's lives. It can affect the primary relationships such as with parents and this can have implications for social interaction and communication throughout life. It is not clear what causes tactile differences though it is speculated that it may be improved by giving oxytocin – the chemical involved in human bonding – which appears to stimulate latent social abilities (Andari *et al.* 2010). Touch, as we established in Chapter 1, is also intrinsically involved in how we assess our environment, we establish its physical parameters and boundaries, what is hot/cold, safe or unsafe. Difficulties in assessing these factors may also have obvious consequences in terms of safety and reassurance. Touch may also affect what we wear. For many people with autism there are certain textures that create extreme discomfort; for example, many people find it difficult to tolerate wool, denim or corduroy, while others find velvet unbearable. This can have implications for the person socially in terms of what they wear. This may be especially the case for adolescents who may want to fit in with their peers through wearing fashionable clothes. They may feel having to wear sweat pants (for example) to every social occasion may decrease social opportunities or indeed inclination to socialise. It may also provide unkind peers opportunity to further isolate them by mocking their choice of attire.

Touch may also have implications in terms of relationships and particularly in terms of sexual relationships, for instance whether the person can tolerate touch or certain types of touch. This may have knock-on effects on the ability of someone with sensory sensitivities to have a sexual relationship, or to find an understanding partner.

There is a variance in how people with ASD tolerate touch, for example Temple Grandin (2006) talks of inventing a hugging machine which she uses to provide strong tactile stimulation. Strong touch is often reassuring for people with ASD, and alternatively light touch can be experienced as uncomfortable or even painful. Some people with tactile differences may have a very high pain threshold which may mean not realising when they have a bad injury or when they have touched something which others would experience as being very hot.

The potential advantages of the myriad sensory differences abound. For example, the ability to withstand pain may be advantageous in certain sports such as boxing, wrestling, MMA (mixed martial arts), rugby or ice hockey, or in certain occupations that are based on physicality such as construction work of any kind, certain types of mining, farming, fishing, horticulture or foundry work (though very rare now). Having tactile differences may include finding certain types of touch deeply pleasurable, for example certain types of sexual contact or particular types of massage.

Many people with sensory differences may derive great pleasure from particular textures or types of clothing.

This pleasure may be beyond what neurotypicals may experience in the same circumstances. This may be an advantage in terms of wearing 'idiosyncratic' clothing. Rather than this being a negative it may, for some, be a positive in establishing a unique look and not feeling pressurised to dress or look a particular way by peers, fashion, popular culture or advertising. This may prove advantageous to those who may wish to forge a career in media, fashion, music or indeed advertising, or for those who wish to remain uninfluenced by the predominant culture.

Vestibular

The vestibular system controls our sense of balance; it takes in and deciphers information about the movement of our head in relation to where we stand/run, etc. It orients us in terms of keeping us upright and in suitable postural positions, and in conjunction with proprioception, it allows us to make calculations as to our body movements in relation to gravity and our environment as well as co-ordinating those movements to allow us to function physically (AOTA 2011). In most people, our vestibular systems work from birth and are intrinsic to the development of parental attachments as the baby learns to move toward the parent for example during feeding and this also lends itself to creating tactile connections. This may mean that babies with vestibular differences may have difficulties in connecting with parents. For most people, however, the vestibular system evolves through our early development and is central to our ability to move independently, beginning with crawling, and as we grow older, we develop the ability to walk independently and gradually add more complex simultaneous movements to our repertoire, such as integrating the visual and vestibular systems in concert with each other to allow these more complex movements or activities.

It is uncertain what creates vestibular differences in people with ASD; however, it is speculated that it is connected to differences in sensory modulation. This theory suggests that many people with ASD are unable to process multiple sensory inputs simultaneously and in the case of vestibular differences, it may mean that the person cannot process the sensory information needed in terms of balance and orientation (Paton *et al.* 2012).

For many people with ASD, vestibular differences may create difficulties in playing sport, or in any other activities that involve orienting the body or limbs, such as rock climbing/ mountain climbing. It may also mean difficulty with stairs, particularly spiral stairs, escalators and lifts. For some people, their vestibular differences may also mean being upside down, or in any other non-upright position, can be problematic, and this may be particularly for children who may not be able to use playground equipment that their neurotypical peers or siblings can use.

Difficulties may also arise on long car journeys where the person may feel vertiginous and nauseous. However, people with vestibular differences that may require sensory inputs will often seek these inputs through activating the vestibular system. This may mean swinging, rocking or moving the head from side to side.

The positive side of vestibular differences can be the pleasure derived from different methods of creating vestibular sensory inputs as just described and in other ways such as riding roller coasters/merry-go-rounds/other amusement rides, fast cars, boats, airplanes or bikes. It may also mean enjoying hang-gliding and gliders.

Proprioception

Proprioception, as described previously, is the perception of the body or limbs in the space that surrounds them.[11] It is what allows for controlled movement, either simple or complex, and in conjunction with the other senses it allows us to orient ourselves and give us a sense of our place within our immediate environments. Proprioception is integral to our development from infancy and works in tandem with our vestibular senses in particular to create a framework of physical identity for us.[12] This means it allows us to automatically understand how our movements are useful to us within our environment; we can use our limbs not only to understand the boundaries of our physical environment but also what is safe and unsafe within this environment. In addition, and also in conjunction with our other senses, it serves to bond us as infants with our caregivers/parents. It does this by allowing us to control the physical movements of our limbs which in turn controls our ability to give and receive tactile information which is integral to emotional/mental/physical infant development (Ayers 2004; Winnicott 1960); it is therefore also very connected to our visual senses as well as our tactile senses. For most infants proprioception works together with other senses to allow them to begin to crawl, stand upright and eventually to walk (Ayers 1979).

Similarly to our vestibular senses, it is as yet unclear why there are proprioceptive differences for people with ASD. It is theorised that it may be to do with an inability to differentiate discrete sensory inputs, or difficulties integrating sensory inputs (local versus global processing) (Paton *et al.* 2012).

---

11 Proprioception is also thought to be involved with general sensory arousal levels and can be important in the regulation of other sensory inputs (Shoener, Kinnealey and Koenig 2008).

12 Our vestibular and proprioceptive senses are combined to become sensory perceptions (Ayers 2004).

It is also theorised that these differences may be to do with a general difficulty in organising sensory information in a way that allows the body to respond/behave appropriately to the inputs.

Having proprioceptive differences can have a huge influence on the lives of many people with ASD. These differences can manifest in difficulties playing sport or doing other physical activities that require a level of sensory integration and/or dexterity. It may also cause 'clumsiness', creating difficulties navigating physical environments as the person may be bumping into objects or people, or standing too close to other people/being unaware of personal space. This can also create social difficulties as others may react badly to being bumped into or feeling that their personal space is being impinged upon. For many people with ASD, being concerned about the reactions of others in social spaces or crowded spaces may also have a limiting effect on their ability to be in these spaces.

There are also positives to having proprioceptive differences. For instance, many people with proprioceptive differences will enjoy climbing, bouncing or jumping. This is often achieved through use of a trampoline but it is also possible for the person to get the proprioceptive inputs they need through sports such as rock climbing, mountain/hill climbing, or running. People with proprioceptive differences may also get necessary inputs from bungees, certain types of swings, some gym equipment but also through some gymnastic activities. Inputs may also be achieved through yoga. For most people with ASD these sensory inputs will be an enjoyable experience and where many people may baulk at the idea of rock climbing, for example, some people with ASD will enjoy the sensations attached to such activities.

Synaesthesia

Synaesthesia as outlined previously describes the ability of an individual to trigger one sense by the stimulation of another. This means that someone may be able to hear colours or see sounds, for example. There is a large number of potential synaesthetic crossings between all the senses, for example tasting colours or hearing shapes. Most commonly these crossings will apply to two senses only but it is also possible to have multi-sensory synaesthesia. The rate of synaesthesia in the general population is thought to be approximately 4 per cent though this figure jumps to 18.9 per cent for people with ASD (Baron-Cohen *et al.* 2013).

Synaesthesia may be broadly divided into two general categories, developmental and acquired. *Developmental synaesthesia* is thought to occur from infancy or birth and appears in clusters so is therefore thought to have a genetic component (Ward and Simner 2005). *Acquired synaesthesia* is induced through external means, usually the use of hallucinogenic drugs. This type of synaesthesia is usually temporary but may also be lasting.

The defining characteristics of synaesthesia are: that the experiences are consciously perceived,[13] they are elicited by processing a sensory stimulus that is not normally associated with that sensory input, they are elicited automatically (not consciously), they are emotional in that they elicit certain emotions in the person experiencing them, synaesthesia is often very difficult for the person experiencing it to describe in words, the experiences are stable and do not tend to change over long periods of time and synaesthesia is memorable in that the synaesthetic sensations/precepts are often more memorable

---

13 There is some debate in philosophy as to whether experiences described as synaesthesia are in fact based on associations rather than perceptions, i.e. whether synaesthetes associate colours with certain sounds or whether colours are distinct from vision (Ross 2008).

than the original sensory stimuli but also it may aid memory generally.

Acquired synaesthesia has a long history that places the experience of differing sensory precepts as being integral to the experience and understanding of the world. This may be termed cultural synaesthesia and is embodied by the Shipibo-Conibo tribe in Peru,[14] for example, who have healing sessions involving the ingestion of the hallucinogenic Ayahuasca by shamans who will then see/hear, etc. the sick person's body and will be able to cure them.[15]

It is not known what causes developmental synaesthesia though it is surmised that it is caused by greater connectivity in certain brain regions which creates pathways not present in non-synaesthetes. In common with other sensory differences in ASD it is also speculated that synaesthesia is associated with difficulties in sensory modulation, in that synaesthetes have difficulty processing the different senses discretely. There is also a genetic theory that links synaesthesia with certain heritable genes (Baron-Cohen *et al.* 2007, 2013). The link between synaesthesia and autism is still being explored genetically (Asher *et al.* 2009) and behaviourally/cognitively (Kemner *et al.* 1995), though single case first-person accounts provide much anecdotal evidence for the links between autism and synaesthesia, most famously in the case of polyglot and mathematician Daniel Tammet. Most recently Baron-Cohen *et al.* (2013) found the rate of synaesthesia amongst an ASD

---

14 The Desana people of Colombia believe that all sensory sensations are connected and associate different colours with different values, for instance red is associated with female fertility, while the sound of a flute is said to be yellow in colour, hot in temperature and masculine in odour.

15 The stimulation of different sensory stimuli during religious, healing or ceremonial occasions is common across many cultures with for example Japanese Buddhist monks hearing incense during prayers.

sample to be 18.9 per cent as opposed to 7.22 per cent in the general population.[16]

There are many advantages to being a synaesthete for people with autism. For instance, the ability to see sounds can be incredibly beneficial for creating music; examples of musicians that describe synaesthetic experiences and how it relates to their creative ability range from Billy Joel to Aphex Twin, from Pharrell Williams to Rimsky-Korsakov.[17] In the world of art, there are many modern and historic synaesthetes from Kandinsky to Carol Steen who have discussed the ways in which synaesthesia has influenced their art.

Many people with synaesthesia also have greater memory recall and this may be useful in a number of contexts, for example in learning languages, remembering numbers, places, things or as a general aid to memory, all of which may be applicable to work or social situations. More than this however is the fact that the vast majority of synaesthetes report their experiences as being very pleasurable. The vividness of these experiences often mirrors the exhilaration that some report when using hallucinogenics (obviously without the inherent health/legal risks). In fact the experience of visual synaesthesia has been likened by many to the experience of being in a pleasant dream. The experience of synaesthesia therefore can often be an emotional experience which creates much pleasure as well as being the source of creativity and having practical, useful implications.

---

16 Baron-Cohen *et al.* 2013 did a research piece on the frequency of synaesthesia in adults with autism using a sample of 172 adults with autism and 123 neurotypical adults.

17 Marks (1978) and Ward *et al.* (2006) have all investigated and written extensively on the connection between vision and music.

CHAPTER 3

The Sense–Memory–Emotion Paradigm

Memory (a quick recap!)

The process of memory is a relatively simple-seeming but complex process which begins in the senses. We use our various senses to interpret the world around us and, in doing so, some of what we are encountering will become important to store in memory as a reference to guide us educationally, physically and emotionally. When we think of memory we classically tend to think of it as being implicated in our ability to remember facts for school, college or work as well as remembering past events. Modern research appears to show that we have a tendency to have greater recall of particular events such as birthday parties due to the heightened significance of such events (being outside of the routine) as well as the potential emotional components of such events.

The process of memory making is:

- From sensory memory[1] to short term which generally lasts less than a minute.

1Also known as iconic memory.

- Short-term memory to long-term memory which potentially lasts a lifetime.

- Long-term memory is then divided into explicit or implicit memory.

The information that is taken in through our senses tends to last milliseconds and is then filed for reference or disappears due to its lack of overall significance. Those who are not visually impaired use their sight as a constant visual record of their surroundings and activities and thus generate masses of information which must then be sifted through for significance. This processing of our surrounds is also what gives our sense of 'now' which appears to last approximately two seconds.[2]

Our relevant sensory memories are converted into short- and then long-term memories depending on what is being processed. The process of memory becoming long term is known as consolidation and this involves the coding and storing of memories which may then be retrieved depending on whether they are processed as implicit (unconscious memories) or explicit (conscious memories). Memories are also subdivided into declarative, which means facts or events, and procedural, which means tasks or skills. Declarative memories are then further divided into episodic or autobiographical memories. Autobiographical memories are thought to be more influenced by emotion[3] and may be defined as being the retrieval of specific events. Research has shown that people generally tend to remember emotional

---

2   Each of these snapshots of 'now' are processed and joined together to give us a sense of continuity. Artists, advertisers and filmmakers in particular use this equation to create continuity of film; if the individual slides/scenes are sped up we lose our ability to process what we are seeing and it consequently stops making sense.

3   Bernstein and Rubin (2002).

events better than neutral events,[4] though people with autism have fewer autobiographical memories than neurotypicals.[5] However, less research has taken place on the type of memories people with autism do retrieve or what situations/ contexts or environments are implicated in their retrieval. Furthermore there has been little research on the connection between how people with autism sensorily perceive certain events or environments at a particular moment and how these perceptions may trigger emotions attached to past events.[6]

Emotion

The connection between memory, emotion and space is often a profound and influential one for those with AS (Tantam 2009). Emotion is very difficult to define given its ambiguous and subjective nature[7] but for the purposes of this chapter we will draw on the Oxford Dictionary definition which describes emotion as involving a feeling, which is distinct from reasoning or knowledge. Emotion can be attached to every activity in our daily lives from the joy some feel at listening to music, to the fear some may feel from being in a fast car, from the anger when someone takes the parking space we have been waiting patiently for, to the contentedness we may feel when we are engrossed in a book. We generally return to activities that give us joy or contentedness as a way of re-experiencing that feeling, though whether we enjoy the same activity every time we do it is subject to many variables.

---

4   Purves, Augustine *et al.* (2008).
5   Crane and Goddard (2008); Crane, Goddard and Pring 2009; Tanweer, Rathbone and Souchay (2010).
6   The connection between senses memory and emotion is an area that is currently still being investigated but requires further research.
7   The Dictionary of Psychology refers to wise authors who avoid direct definitions and instead tease out what emotion is through their writing.

For instance, a walk along the beach on a clement day may be a very satisfying experience while a walk along the same beach on a stormy day may be challenging, uncomfortable or even frightening.

There has been a long-standing stereotype of people with autism as being un-emotional and robotic. This may stem from a public misconception of some clinical writing which has placed a lack of empathy as being a central feature of autism and has led to a confusion in the media in particular which has equated lack of empathy with lack of emotion. This has influenced the perception of autism and is often the main focus of fictional portrayals of autism in movies and books and it is often explicitly or implicitly framed as being a contributory factor in unfortunate news stories attributing autism to people who have just committed crimes which in turn generates a particular damaging perspective of autism in the general public. This does not just take place in the mainstream news; it is also prevalent online with much damaging rhetoric written about people with autism and their ability to feel emotion.

Even a cursory glance at the autobiographical work of Gunilla Gerland, Donna Williams, Lianne Holliday Willey or Naoki Higashida shows the depth of emotion that these authors with autism have or are experiencing. Naoki Higashida (2013), for example, discusses the experience of 'flashback memories' in which the recollection of a bad memory creates a flood of emotion which takes him back to the original feelings he had when the memory was being created.[8]

As noted in Chapter 1, from a scientific point of view it is important to understand that we are still very much in the phase of learning about the brain and about emotion.

---

8   This is termed mood-dependent memory.

What has become increasingly clear is the plasticity of the brain and its ability to adapt if certain parts are damaged or different. This realisation has also meant there has been a re-appraisal of the ways we have understood the brain to work and in particular the function of different parts of the brain. However, it is generally accepted that there are three key parts of the brain involved with emotion and memory; these are the amygdala, the hypothalamus and the hippocampus.

Emotion has two components: conscious emotions which are relayed through the cerebral cortex and involve planning, reasoning, etc., and unconscious emotion which is relayed through the amygdala. The amygdala receives information about a situation and the ways the body has reacted to it then generates an emotion attached to this; the hypothalamus regulates that emotion. The hippocampus stores long-term memories and the memory of emotions. It is thought that the amygdala works differently for people with autism in that sensory information bypasses the conscious and goes straight to unconscious and thus bypasses reasoning. In general the amygdala is central to both the retrieval of memories and also the re-experiencing of those memories from an emotional perspective.[9]

Sense–memory–emotion

Buchanan (2007) and Purves, Augustine *et al.* (2008) talk about memory retrieval and re-experiencing emotions when triggered by reminders of the events that caused these emotions initially. Given that our perception is informed in the first instance by our senses, people often retrieve a memory and re-experience

---

9   Buchanan (2007).

an emotion on the basis of the senses, particularly through the sense of smell.[10]

Many people with autism have reported the experience of a particular smell or sound in a contemporary space which reminds them of negative spaces in the past. For example, some people with autism have talked about the sights, sounds and smells of busy spaces being evocative of school spaces. This is often negatively re-experienced as a significant proportion of people with autism recall their school days negatively. Most research and literature on sensory differences and experiences for people with autism tends to focus on neuroscientific explanations rather than exploring the experience from an emotional point of view. In other words it may be interesting to approach the issues of sensory experiences from the perspective of the person experiencing/feeling them. If a person with autism re-experiences negative feelings from the past which are associated with a particular space, rather than only attributing this to sensory differences in the contemporary space it may be worth looking at the fact that there may be difficult memories associated with the experience of different senses.

As an example, if a person with autism is in a busy café and the noisy hubbub of that café is evocative of a noisy classroom in a school that the person was bullied in, then it is not just a sensory difficulty that the person is experiencing in that moment; it is the memory of past experiences that is retrieved by the triggering of the senses through a particular stimuli. This warrants further investigation as the assumption may often be that in this scenario the difficulties the person is experiencing in the busy café are to do with their

---

10 It seems clear that for example smell and memory are closely linked with approximately two to three synapses separating the amygdala and the olfactory bulb.

hyper-sensitivity to sounds rather than the sounds triggering an emotional memory.

The potential significance of examining the sensory–memory–emotional perspective for people with autism is that it represents a different understanding of sensory difficulties. Rather than only looking at how the person is experiencing sensory difficulties in that moment, it is also worth taking a more holistic/life course approach that takes into consideration aspects of the individual's past experiences that play a part in their present. Exploring the past emotional experiences that may cause or exacerbate sensory experiences in the present also acknowledges the difficulties people may have with contextualising and dealing with the memories of bad experiences. For example, this interviewee describes the difficulty associated with school and how those difficulties reverberate through his lifetime in other contexts:

> When you are very uncomfortable for three years in a certain kind of environment that environment will always bring that uncomfortableness with it…and you see echoes of that environment in other environments.
>
> (Interviewee A)

Though the difficulties associated with having autism may be a contributory factor in these bad experiences for some (for example, stimming or other manifestations of the person's autism may lead to ostracisation or bullying, particularly in school), this should not deny or preclude the person experiencing them from the same level of empathy and understanding that we would afford a neurotypical who has had the same experiences. It stands to reason that if a person with autism has had emotionally difficult experiences in particular situations or spaces, these experiences will affect them in the same way as they would affect neurotypicals who have the same experiences, yet it seems the emphasis remains on the person's autism, and this in some ways, one could argue, is to deny the person their humanity by focusing on a diagnosis or on 'deficits'.

ASD and the sense–memory–emotion paradigm: a strategy

Having looked at the ways in which the sense–memory–emotion paradigm may affect people with autism, we will now turn our attention to what strategy they may be able to employ in order to manage these effects. Primarily, the issues we have described here are issues of the past still being experienced in the present. For anyone experiencing what we will describe as legacy issues, the primary way they may choose to try and address them is through talk therapy. This can be a relatively contentious method for people with autism. There are many reasons for this. For example, many will find the idea of discussing past issues with a 'stranger' a difficult proposition. They may find the prospect too intimidating due to anxiety or they may find it difficult to articulate how they feel about these issues. They may also find the idea of revisiting these emotions to be an unwelcome proposition; it may be that they would prefer to move on and forget. However, we would argue that the use of counselling therapy will often be an integral part of a person's Sensory Strategy. The strategy should contain practical ways in which the person manages their sensory environment, but it should also, if necessary, look to counselling as a way of dealing with the emotional residue that may be attached to certain spaces – in this instance a practical strategy alone may not be entirely sufficient in meeting their needs.

One of the biggest difficulties for many people with ASD in finding a counsellor will be fear and procrastination. This can often mean that though the person with autism recognises the potential benefits in getting counselling, they may find the thoughts of having to find a counsellor sufficiently anxiety-inducing as to prevent them from doing so. This is often a case of being stuck in the 'thinking' phase and never arriving at the 'doing' phase. The journey from thinking to doing may feel as if it is blocked, that there is a barrier to 'doing'. This is usually anxiety based and can be addressed through breaking the task into component parts, writing them out if necessary, so that each component part can become a mini-achievement in itself, with a view towards building to a whole. It is important to try and stay within a time schedule as regards completing the task. If the process continues for too long it can mean too much time spent in the contemplation (thinking) stage and not enough in the action (doing) stage. If necessary it may be worthwhile for the person to have a trusted other, a family member, spouse/partner or support worker, help them in finding a counsellor.

In order to best meet the individual needs of a person with autism in the counselling setting it is very important to first find the right counsellor. This may mean trial and error; we cannot be entirely prescriptive as to what encapsulates the right counsellor as people will individually have different requirements and needs from their counsellor. What may be useful as a general framework though is that the counsellor should be someone that the person feels they can talk openly with, and who will be able to help the person to do so. Ideally the counsellor should have an understanding of autism and be able to assist clients in articulating themselves through the use of different means – for example, encouraging the client to articulate themselves through writing, or through recording their voice and sending this to the counsellor to be then discussed at subsequent sessions. The counsellor's office should ideally be relatively easy to access for the client; this means that the client should arrive for their session with a relatively low level of anxiety. It also stands to reason that the counsellor's office should be sensorily comfortable. This means un-intrusive lighting, noises, colours, ambience, patterns or smells.

The following chapters will focus on the specific sensory differences and difficulties that people with autism may experience and will explore the different spaces and contexts of people's lives in which these sensory differences or difficulties have an impact. We will also include the sense–memory–emotion paradigm as part of our exploration of the sensory experiences of people with autism. The first section of this exploration will focus on school.

CHAPTER 4

School and College Spaces

School

As previously stated, school may present many difficulties for people with autism. School represents the first site of social interaction and the first real engagement with public space for most. For a proportion of people with ASD this experience may be dominated by negative interactions with peers and an uncomfortable introduction to public spaces. Much of this negativity may come in the form of peer victimisation or bullying, and this may have the knock-on effect of negatively shaping their first real experience of public space: 'not everyone on the spectrum was bullied but most were and what bullying did occur was likely felt more strongly because of the individual's inability to understand why it was happening in the first place' (Carley 2008, p.87).

There is bullying in all schools (Bond *et al.* 2001); however, people with ASDs are at a higher risk of victimisation and bullying than the general populace (Roekel, Scholte and Didden 2010). Some of the reasons why those with ASDs may be at higher risk of bullying and victimisation revolve around the difficulties they may have with social interaction, initiating and maintaining friendships (Bauminger and Kasari 2000), and repetitive behaviours (Haq and Le Couteur 2004).

One of the primary aspects of mainstream society is the cultural reproduction of sameness and 'normality' (Kitchin 1998). This serves to delineate between those 'insiders' who fit in with 'norms' and those outsiders who are discriminated against and isolated from social spaces (Hall 2004). Given that 'outsider' status is bestowed on anyone who does not fit in with cultural 'norms', people with ASD who often exhibit 'odd' or 'unusual' behaviours in public spaces (Holliday Willey 1999) find themselves in this category. The expectations of sameness and 'normality' are often difficult for people with ASD to abide by, not only because of the manifestations of their ASD but also because they often don't understand the expectations in the first place. As Goffman (1963a, p.45) states in relation to those who are 'othered' and stigmatised: 'One phase of this socialisation process is that through which the stigmatized person learns and incorporates the stand point of the normal'. This quote from Goffman is also applicable to the desire of people with ASD to try and fit in by learning the ways in which they can behave like 'insiders'. This is often a learned and performed charade on the part of the individual with ASD who may not understand the rules of so-called 'normal' behaviour (Moloney 2010), but may understand that they must attempt to fit in with mainstream society (Goffman 1963b).

For people with autism who have sensory difficulties, there may be associated coping mechanisms that they use, such as removing themselves from spaces that are problematic (as with the example that follows of the person who spent most break times in the toilet) or stimming. For many people on the AS, 'stimming' or self-stimulatory behaviour is a response to anxiety, and may be particularly manifest in public spaces.

'Stimming' activities may include hand flapping, rocking or spinning and they serve to soothe people on the AS in situations where they feel anxious (Simone 2010) but they also serve to draw more attention to the person's lack of ability to fit in with the 'norm'. This is exemplified by Interviewee G who says:

> when I was being bullied obviously my behaviour that would have been drastically different to everyone else around me. I came across as being odd, as being different and I was picked out for that and it was very stressful at the time.

The interviewee was excluded from the mainstream communal spaces of the school because of his perceived lack of understanding or unwillingness to conform to expectations of 'normal' behaviour. The school epitomises the learning ground for social 'norms'. These 'norms' are often reinforced by schools whose strict guidelines for behaviour simultaneously 'other' and exclude the person with an ASD by placing their behaviour outside of the 'norm', which may also legitimise the victimisation and bullying by fellow pupils.

These negative first experiences of a public space may reverberate through time and into contemporary public spaces for many with autism (the sense–memory–emotion paradigm); therefore many people with autism may associate the transition from the relative safety of childhood and the home space to the potential anxiety of later childhood and adolescence and its associations with larger, busier public spaces. The secondary school experience in particular may cause reverberations throughout the lives of people with autism. Many people with autism have talked about spending all the time between classes in the bathroom due to the sensory difficulties inherent in busy school corridors including crowds, fluorescent lighting, certain smells and patterns of floor tiles. For this interviewee, the anxiety and sensory stresses attached to the school environment eventually led to them withdrawing completely from school and isolating themselves at home:

> I made myself keep going and I achieved a very high baseline of awkwardness and near panic at all times from school which impacted on my health after a year and a half…it reached a point where my health was being affected to such a state that I had something of a breakdown in second year so I gradually became more of a hermit as I tried to come into school…eventually any kind of motivation or energy that I had left and I was inert at home for five years or so.

This is an example of how sensory stresses and social anxiety can combine to create a withdrawal for some people with autism from public spaces. This in turn has repercussions for the person educationally, in terms of work, in terms of social development and most importantly in terms of mental health. The isolation and loneliness many people with autism feel when they have withdrawn from social spaces may be acute. In many instances there is a direct line from the person's sensory issues to the impacts on their daily lives and their mental health.

The physical environment of school and college

There are a number of ways in which the school or college environment can create difficulties for people with autism. These include: lighting, flooring, the structure of school spaces, auditory factors, quiet spaces, sensory rooms and class furniture.

In terms of *lighting* it is common for people with sensory difficulties to hear a hum from fluorescent lighting which may be very distracting for them, especially in a classroom situation where it might be very difficult to listen to the teacher or lecturer when this distracting hum is ever present.

Patterns found in *flooring*, in the form of different coloured tiling (particularly if it is not in a set geometric pattern) – for example, blue tiles on a white floor – may be disconcerting for the person. This may be especially true in busy spaces such as corridors where the person's anxiety may already be raised.

Narrow corridors between classrooms may be prohibitive for people with ASD. These spaces may contain a number of sensory difficulties including the noises of crowds of students, the smells associated with crowds and the potential for people to be in very close proximity or touching against each other.

There may be sensory difficulties around a number of spaces in the school or college associated with *auditory* inputs. As well as the noises in corridors there may also be noises in gymnasiums or any other sporting arenas (this includes team and spectator noises that are generally present in outdoor field sports).

Creating a better sensory architecture in school and college

Given the social and cultural importance of school in the lives of most children and adolescents, it is vital that the environment be conducive to allowing people with ASD to have the same opportunities to learn as neurotypicals. In order for that to happen there needs to be a recognition on the part of schools to provide a learning environment suitable to the needs of people with autism. This means taking a flexible, creative and individualised approach to supporting students. Central to this approach should be a consideration for the sensory needs of students with ASD. Taking these needs into consideration and creating an appropriate environment from them is not just an issue of policy; it should also be a moral imperative based on the notions of equity and acceptance of diversity.

There are many specific ways in which schools/colleges should take the sensory needs of people with autism into account. For instance, in the built environment schools should be cognisant of creating inclusive spaces. Traditionally this has meant universal design – which, while welcome, usually takes into consideration physical difficulties students (or staff) may experience rather than other difficulties such as sensory difficulties. This, then, means that many school spaces are not inclusive for all but contain areas that, through their sensory implications, may be exclusive for some. This is also true for colleges though the relative freedom that college students have somewhat offsets this issue (we will discuss college issues in more detail later).

The starting point in the creation of an inclusive sensory architecture should include an understanding of the varying sensory needs of people with autism. This means taking into consideration that each individual may be hyper- as well as hypo-sensitive depending on the stimuli. It also means taking into consideration that each person may experience a greater manifestation of their sensory issues depending on the level of anxiety they are experiencing at a given time. Therefore consideration should be given to the part anxiety plays in the person's sensory experiences (and vice versa) as well as what the reasons behind this anxiety may be. It is impossible to separate out the sensory issues as being a problem to be addressed in isolation without taking into account the other factors (such as anxiety) associated with the sensory issues or directly causing the sensory issues.

The creation of an inclusive sensory architecture should begin with an individualised 'learning plan' for each student.

This plan should be tailored to meet the needs of each student and should be based on a person-centred approach where the student's needs are primary and all supports are designed to promote those needs. The plan should be created at the beginning of each school year and should be reviewed and revised on a yearly basis (or more frequently if necessary). The plan should be a comprehensive document that outlines all the needs of the student in order to best allow them to thrive in the school environment. As previously stated this means that the various difficulties the person may experience are addressed including anxiety, social needs as well as a specific sensory plan. The process of creating the Learning Plan should involve a multi-disciplinary approach with the student, teachers, parents, Special Needs Assistants, Learning Support Officers, Disability Officers, Occupational Therapists or any other relevant supports for the student being part of the process. The plan should include the following:

- A written/visual schedule should be written up incorporating subject/times and classroom numbers.

- Where possible each teacher should set out what will be covered in the subject at the start of each year and at the beginning of each class.

- Teachers should use 'key concepts' which would serve as a framework for understanding of what will be covered in each class; these would ideally be given in bullet point form.

- A set of rules/guidelines should be individually created that would set out how to ask questions in class, how to approach a teacher, what is appropriate in the classroom space (e.g. music, playing games/using phones during the lecture); these could be written and given to the student so they can refer to them as need be.

- The student should be made aware of break times and lunch times, bringing in food or eating in the student canteen/dining area. Consider the possibility of having a peer/buddy system for break times, where the student is shown where to go or who will stay with them at break times.

- If the student has an issue with a subject/topic/teacher, they should have a liaison that they can approach who will provide guidance to them on these issues; this may be the Special Needs Assistant (SNA), a tutor, Learning Support Officer or preferred teacher.

- This person needs to take the lead in terms of assisting the student to liaise with staff.

- The student may need to be able to record each class by using voice-recording equipment.

- The student should be encouraged to use a diary but also prompts/reminders through their mobile phone and Google calendars, etc.

- The student should have a study plan created in conjunction with the Learning Support Officer/SNA.

- If there are any disruptive behaviours/outbursts/ meltdowns in class these should be discussed individually with the student outside of the classroom hall and ideally involving the students' liaison.

- The student should be supported socially through a peer-mentoring programme.

- The school should consider setting up an ASD support group; this may take the form of peer support from older students with ASD.

Specific sensory needs

- The creation of a learning plan should take into consideration the sensory needs of the student.

- This should be individually tailored and should include optimum amount of time per study period, use of music/other sensory stimuli, use of auditory/visual aids.

- The plan should also include pre-emptive sensory breaks (rather than waiting until the person is nearing sensory overload or has a meltdown).

- There should be a sensory room which includes the equipment necessary to meet the sensory needs of students (either hypo or hyper).

This plan is also applicable to the college environment with the same needs arising in similar spaces.

The learning plan aims to take into account all the needs of the person with autism. It is not possible to address the sensory needs of the person in isolation from their other needs. However, it is imperative that there is a specific sensory plan which seeks to address the individual needs of each student. The sensory plan is somewhat predicated on the resources and the will of each school. For instance, there are schools that are better resourced and therefore will have a comprehensive list of equipment in a sensory room, while other schools may have a nominal 'sensory room' which is an empty room that students with autism are sent to when feeling overwhelmed. There are ways to work within an under-resourced system and still provide sensory supports to students with autism. For example, having pre-emptive sensory breaks can be very helpful for students with ASD. This means building a structure into the student's curriculum that allows them to feed their sensory needs before/between/taking time outs from classes where possible in order to allow them to concentrate in or tolerate the classroom environment (in terms of resources it may be possible to have minimal equipment in order to meet some of the students sensory needs, such as Velcro, rubber balls or music as examples of inexpensive but very useful sensory props). It is common for students with ASD to get these breaks only when they are already overwhelmed and this may just add to social difficulties the person is experiencing if they have a 'meltdown' or run out of class.

The difficulty for many students is whether they themselves recognise the signs that they are becoming overwhelmed, and how to address this. One way of addressing this issue is by having watches, etc. that can monitor the rate of heartbeat, in this way they can begin (with support) to recognise the signs of rising heart rate and the potential for 'meltdown'. This may allow the student to take pre-emptive steps to address this before it happens. Another method may be for the student to have a temperature chart (with white on one end signifying calm, through a spectrum of colours to red at the other end signifying 'meltdown'). With support the student may be able to use this chart as a way of recognising the warning signs and pre-empt greater difficulties. This chart can be in the student's individual journal or can be on the wall of the classroom where it can be used for all the students in the class, regardless of having autism or not. A final suggestion is based on a similar principle as the colour chart, where instead of colours there is a simple number chart with 1 signifying calm and 10 signifying 'meltdown'. The student should be supported in using these visual methods to identify potential difficulties for themselves; however, if possible this should not be done in lieu of pre-emptive sensory breaks.

These visual methods generally work best for students that are hypo-sensitive. For students that are hyper-sensitive it may be the overstimulation of the school or college spaces that creates difficulties for them. This may be addressed by having specific work areas that are designed (as much as is practical in a classroom setting) to limit the amount of inputs the person has to contend with. This may mean that there are still visual cues but that they are in a self-contained area for the student rather than the student having to open up their senses to the potentially overwhelming variety of inputs contained in the classroom. The excellent National Autistic Society website suggests dividing classrooms up into individual work areas as discussed above but also that classrooms should be divided into work or leisure/play areas also so that students have very clear definitions of what each space is for and also that they may be able to take breaks if necessary.

Specific college needs

Though we have looked at the creation of a sensory architecture and a Learning Plan which addresses the sensory needs of students with autism for schools as well as colleges, there are specific sensory issues related to college which we will explore. The physical environment of the average college campus is usually a little different from the school campus. It is usually bigger, with more students and more activity around its physical environs. This may be in contrast with many schools where there are set times for classes which are delineated chunks of time spent generally in a relatively quiet classroom, without the distraction of hundreds or thousands of students milling about outside. This represents a certain predictability that many people with autism appreciate. In contrast the college campus will generally have swathes of people moving about at all times during the academic year and this can be distracting or even distressing for many people with autism. It means that even in a relatively sensory free lecture hall, external sensory inputs can impact on the student's anxiety. A further potential difference between school and college is contained within the lecture halls themselves. Many are vast containing hundreds of students. This is seen as a positive by many with autism in that there is the possibility of 'disappearing' in a larger class cohort and therefore less likelihood of feeling like you 'stand out'. The potential downside of the larger lecture halls is that hundreds of people in an interior bounded space bring with them the potential of a variety of sights, sounds, smells and tactile implications that may be distressing for many people with ASD.

A further difference is that the relative freedom of student life, as referred to earlier, also brings with it some anxieties. The clear chunks of time represented by each class in school is easily followed and becomes part of a routine that many find comforting. In college it is expected that the student will orient themselves with the campus and negotiate their own timetables in order to be on time for each lecture. This means knowing the physical layout of the campus which will usually mean having to walk in spaces filled with people (indoor or outdoor) and this may have sensory implications. The knock-on effects of this may be that the student arrives for their lecture already quite anxious or beginning to feel sensorily overwhelmed. This may then affect the student's ability to take in what is being said in the lecture and may also discourage the student if they feel they have to run this gamut each time they move between lectures. This example serves as a way of understanding how potentially significant sensory issues may be for people with ASD but also how it is not possible to discuss sensory issues in isolation from the rest of the person's life.

There are also positive sensory implications from college life. One of these is the proliferation of societies that most colleges contain. These societies/clubs serve many tastes and interests but what they may also do is allow students with ASD to address sensory issues through the use of certain physical activities. This may be a very useful outlet as many people with autism do not want to feel different or to stand out from their peers. The use of societies or clubs may allow people with sensory differences to have their needs met without drawing attention to themselves. In Chapter 2 we looked at the potential for certain physical activities to meet the sensory needs of people with autism. Examples of these include rock climbing, mountain climbing, hang gliding, cycling or certain combat sports. Most of these activities and many others that are similar will be found in college clubs and societies.

College social spaces

College contains many social spaces that may be either challenging or useful for people with ASD. In the previous section we looked at an example of useful spaces in terms of clubs and societies that may serve to meet some of the sensory needs of people with autism. It is very important to note that these clubs and societies may also create social opportunities for people with autism. They are based on a specific activity which means they are generally task focused, may provide sensory outlets and usually do not require intense one-to-one communication inherent in other social situations which many people with ASD may find intimidating or off-putting.

There are also many challenging social spaces for people with sensory difficulties on college campus. The most prominent of these are the pub or club. College often represents the first real exertion of adult independence, a movement away from the sheltering safety/familiarity of family or the family home and an opportunity to begin to fully develop our identities.

Inherent in this process is the expectation amongst many students that college will provide opportunities to make friends, to socialise with others and much of this socialisation takes place in pubs or clubs. For many people with autism who have sensory issues pubs and clubs contain many difficulties that can create anxiety or prevent the person from going to these spaces. What is often more difficult is that there is an expectation amongst a large proportion of students that most people attending college will go to pubs or clubs. This social expectation can create anxieties for people with ASD who may feel on the one hand that this is how people socialise and in order to fit in with that, they should go, while on the other hand these spaces may create significant sensory issues for them. In the following chapter we will explore how people with autism interact with public spaces which may contain sights, sounds or smells that may be distracting or distressing for them.

CHAPTER 5

The Sensory Implications of Public Spaces, Social Spaces and Work Spaces

Many people with AS experience sensory difficulties (Gerland 2006; Grandin 2007; Shore 2003; Williams 1992). Sensory difficulties may revolve around any of the senses and tend to manifest most frequently in public spaces. This is because these spaces in particular contain a variety of sights, sounds and smells that may overload the senses of an individual with AS. For example, Interviewee A talks about his experiences of heightened senses in public spaces:

> I, well when I said I was normal at home. I'm generally normal kind of, I wouldn't be sensitive to things, but when I go out in public, depending on how uncomfortable I am, I notice sounds – behind me especially – I will be put on edge by them, by movement, peripheral vision movement. I will be noticing smells and sometimes when I am in a chair I will be kind of distracting myself with the texture of it.

The experience of being in a public space heightens the interviewee's awareness of, and sensitivity to, movement, noises and smells. There is a direct correlation for him between how anxious he feels and how sensitive he becomes to sensory inputs. It is not, in his opinion, that he has improved sensory abilities in these instances, but rather his 'attention to them' (Interviewee A) has increased. In moments of anxiety in public spaces he becomes acutely aware of the minutiae of the sensory geography of that space. The distraction of examining the texture of his chair may be a form of 'stimming'.

As mentioned in the last chapter, social spaces such as clubs, bars and cafés can be sensorily problematic for people with ASD. This can have knock-on effects in many facets of the lives of people with sensory issues. For example, given the previously stated preference of many to do most of their socialising through pubs and clubs, opportunities for socialising may be hampered for those who find these spaces difficult to be in. This in turn can have a shrinking effect on the world of people with ASD. The less someone is socialising with others, the more difficult it may be to develop social skills/social awareness and the more likelihood of isolation.

Pubs

Pubs are spaces created to allow people to socialise and imbibe in a convivial atmosphere which may include live music, karaoke, darts, pool or other forms of entertainment. They are also businesses with a money-making imperative and most will do what is necessary to increase the amount of customers they have even if this means that the pub may become uncomfortable for people who are not drinking alcohol. For instance, in many pubs after a certain hour, the volume of music is increased in order to promote more drinking as conversation becomes more difficult. Also the more alcohol people imbibe the less aware they become of their proximity to others or, to put it another way, of others' personal space. Therefore there are numerous sensory implications of pubs that are influenced by the type of pub, for example whether it is busy or quiet at certain times or all the time, whether it has music or other forms of entertainment, how big the pub is and whether it has air conditioning.

Interviewee A talks about feeling obliged to go to the pub as it serves as a form of socialising with friends/others. In situations where he is able to meet in a 'quiet' pub he is able to speak with his companions and does not generally find that there are many sensory implications for him. However, if he is in a busy pub he feels that he is unable to interact with others as he is too distracted by the various sights, sounds and smells that surround him. In these situations he has a tendency to concentrate on the television if there is one and is generally 'tuned out' from the conversation. Interviewee C similarly describes the experience of being in a busy pub as uncomfortable. He also finds it extremely difficult to interact with others and finds it very difficult to pick out the threads of conversation between friends, because of the background din that is generally contained in a pub. This can be a demoralising experience for many as it discourages them from going to a pub, or it may create huge difficulties socially interacting with others even if they do go to the pub.

Nightclubs

While pubs vary in terms of potential sensory inputs, nightclubs generally do not. Nightclubs play music, they serve alcohol and promote the idea of close physical proximity or other forms of physical expression namely through dancing. This means that there are more potential sensory issues contained in a nightclub than a pub. For many people the nightclub is where they go to dance, drink alcohol or meet others for sexual/relationships purposes. People often go to these clubs after the pub or after imbibing/ingesting alcohol or other substances in house parties. This means that people are often even less aware of their own physical presence or the personal space of others than in pubs. Nightclubs also have certain expectations for some in that they expect to meet others for potential dalliances (or dances!). This may create added anxiety for many people with ASD (though many people with autism happily go to nightclubs and experience minimal anxiety or sensory issues).

Further sensory issues may include strobe lighting or vibrant lighting effects creating sensory visual difficulties, though the opposite may also be true in that people with ASD may also really enjoy the visuals as a method of stimulation. For most, however, the combination of the visuals, the noise of the music which is generally extremely loud in nightclubs, the noise of the crowds, the proximity to others and the social expectation create a sense-scape that is potentially very problematic and difficult to manage. Allied to the difficulties as laid out above there is often an expectation of dancing which also brings its own potential sensory issues. For example, people with tactile issues may find it uncomfortable to be in contact with others – particularly transient contact as opposed to deep pressure. Also in the case of Interviewee C he feels he gets overstimulated by any physical contact with others and often becomes inadvertently aroused which creates uncomfortable situations for him. People with vestibular and/or proprioceptive difficulties may also find dancing either a challenge or an enjoyable sensory input.

Supermarkets

Supermarkets bring many of the same sensory challenges as pubs or nightclubs; they contain noises, sights and smells that many will find difficult to contend with. However, there are some differences between supermarkets and social spaces in that there are specific issues in supermarkets that many people with autism find particularly difficult.

Let's take a scenario where someone with ASD and sensory issues enters a supermarket. The first sensory issue that they may find difficult is the noise from the checkouts which are generally at the front of the supermarket. For instance, Interviewee B talks about how the beeping from the checkout as each item's barcode is scanned can be experienced on a scale from uncomfortable to distressing depending on how anxious she feels. The second sensory issue may be the squeaking noise from some shopping trolley wheels as they are moved around the supermarket. The third potential sensory issue may be the cacophony of noises emanating from other shoppers such as children crying/shouting, parents crying/shouting (!) and announcements from tannoy systems that are often set at a very loud volume and/or are preceded by a high-pitched beeping. The fourth potential sensory issue may be the low-pitched hum of fluorescent lighting which is relatively ubiquitous in supermarkets. The fifth potential sensory issue is the variety of competing aromas in supermarkets. This runs the gamut from the carefully placed smells of bread baking near the entrance of supermarkets to the meat or fish counters at the rear, all competing with the various scents people use on themselves including strong aftershave, perfume and deodorant. Taking all of these potential sensory issues into consideration, the supermarket can be a very daunting experience for many people with sensory issues. What sets the supermarket apart from social spaces such as cafés, pubs and nightclubs is the necessity for most people to use the supermarket. In other words spaces designed for social interaction such as pubs and clubs – while extremely important – are not vital in the way buying provisions is. Using the supermarket is also intrinsic to being independent for most people and therefore is often seen as a 'necessary evil' by many people with autism.

Streets

Streets are the arteries of our towns and cities. They have shops, supermarkets, restaurants and pubs but are also conduits between different locations meaning they not only serve commercial purposes but also vital infrastructural purposes. Streets can be experienced differently as they change from the more commercial/infrastructural functions of day-time into the more entertainment-focused functions of night-time. This means that streets are multi-functional and temporally influenced and therefore have a vast array of sensory stimulants. The first of these is the crowds of people particularly in bigger towns or cities or in more tourist-friendly places. For most towns or cities, weekends, holidays and night-times generally tend to be their busiest times. This means there are likely to be more people shopping during the day-time and socialising during the night-time. For people with sensory issues there are a number of sensory implications of streets that are busy. There are the noises of the crowds (talking, shouting, crying, laughing, children) which can be overwhelming, especially on narrow streets where people are in close proximity to each other, and there may be echoes or amplification because of the physical structure of the street. There are also the noises of the businesses that ply their trades on the street. For instance, there may be loud music from shops in the day-time and pubs/clubs at night-time, there may also be noises (and fumes!) from traffic such as beeping horns or loud car stereos. For people with tactile issues there is the potential for people to brush against each other in busier streets and this can be an uncomfortable and off-putting experience. At night-time there is the added possibility of this happening if people are consuming alcohol and therefore less aware of personal space. There are also many visual components to the street in terms of strobe lighting, for example, which some people may find uncomfortable. It is the combination of all these sensory components that generally makes streets an uncomfortable space or even an overwhelming space for people with sensory difficulties.

Travel

The purpose of travel may vary from leisure to necessity, from going on a holiday or travelling the world to going to work or visiting family. The common ground between the different reasons for travelling are the methods by which we do so, for example plane, boat, train or car.

Airports/trains, planes and automobiles

Airports have a similar sense-scape as busy streets or supermarkets. They contain noises of people, tannoys and entertainment, for example. They do differ, however, in that as well as all the potential sensory issues that other spaces contain, airports are larger and therefore have even more people noises as well as having the potential tactile implications of busy streets. They also differ in the general atmosphere of airports which is often imbued with anxiety and stress as people try to gather luggage, check in, and go through security checks in time to make their flights. For people with tactile sensory issues whose anxiety may already be heightened in an airport, the experience of having to go through rigorous security checks which usually include being patted down can be a distressing experience. Many people with autism have spoken about how their heightened anxiety can arouse suspicion among security staff and therefore make them more likely to be singled out to be searched.

Having got through the airport experience and boarded a plane, there may be more sensory issues to contend with. For example, the 'airless' atmosphere on a plane has been spoken about by people with autism as creating anxiety. This is allied with the move towards smaller seats and more passengers on many modern airlines which means closer proximity to fellow passengers and hence potential sensory tactile difficulties.

The issues outlined previously as regards airports and planes also apply to train stations, trains (though many people with ASD prefer train journeys as there is generally more room and there is space to get up and walk around), and bus stations. Buses and getting the Tube, however, often create specific tactile sensory difficulties for many people with ASD due to the potential for overcrowding, having to stand, as well as vestibular difficulties from the movement of these vehicles – particularly the swaying motion that often accompanies these journeys. This may also apply to boat trips.

Work

Similarly to school and college spaces, workplaces may bring a variety of sensory implications for people with sensory issues. However, before looking at the sensory issues associated with different workplaces we should begin by looking at the process of getting a job in the first instance and specifically how to manage the sensory implications of a job interview.

If you are lucky enough to have a job interview it is imperative to do all in your power to take as much of the anxiety out of the situation as possible. This begins with finding out about your potential employers, what is their business, their philosophy and what would the job you are applying for entail. It is always wise to practise job interviews beforehand with trusted friends/family members or professionals/support workers. This may involve role playing and getting the person to ask you a series of questions. Though you cannot anticipate every question that will be asked, you can anticipate certain questions and be prepared for them, for example:

- Why do you want the job?

- What skills can you bring to your potential employer?

- Can you work in a team as well as under your own initiative?

It may also be worthwhile having a question prepared for your potential employer as most will allow you space at the end of the interview to ask a question. This would be a good opportunity to use some of the knowledge/research you have about the company to ask a pertinent question and show you have prepared well for the interview. When preparing for the job interview it is also a good idea to take notes on what you are researching. This will assist in terms of memory retention and will also allow you to go back over what you have written prior to doing the interview.

Part of the preparation for a job interview should be a consideration of the logistics of the interview. This should include how you are going to get to the interview site at the allotted time. Take your sensory needs into consideration when planning this. If, for example, you find buses to be a difficult sensory environment then either get the quietest bus you can or look at another method of getting to the interview site. What is not recommended is that you put yourself in a situation where you are incredibly stressed due to whatever sensory environment you have been in on the way to the interview. It is worth looking at the job interview site on Google Earth/Google Maps and familiarise yourself with its location and how to get there. If possible it is a good idea to do a trial run prior to the interview date, i.e. use whatever method of transport that you will be using on the day and time yourself doing it. Allow for the fact that it is good practice to turn up early for job interviews. How early is a matter for each of us individually; it is not a good idea to be an hour early as this may just mean sitting with other nervous candidates in a potentially warm office! Ten to fifteen minutes early is a sensible amount of time.

In terms of the interview itself, it is a good idea to think about what clothes to wear on the day. These need to be smart for most job interviews but they also need to be comfortable for you to wear. This means not causing any sensory discomfort through itchy material, for instance. It is also a good idea to cut the tags off the clothes after you have bought them as many people with ASD and sensory issues find tags to be very uncomfortable. If you are buying new clothes for the job interview make sure to try them on first so you can avoid the issues outlined above.

Be prepared for the possibility that the interview site will usually be in an office. This means the likelihood of fluorescent lighting, air conditioning which means extra noise or no air conditioning which may mean a stuffy and warm office. If possible when you arrive for your interview and after you have checked in with the office administrator/secretary, take the opportunity to go to the bathroom and compose yourself. Take a couple of minutes (no more than two or three minutes) to relax yourself, and begin to acclimatise yourself with the sensory environment of the office.

When you enter the room for the job interview shake hands with your interviewer(s), and try to answer the questions being asked in a practical way. This means neither being too effusive or answering in monosyllables. Take into consideration that if the waiting area of the interview is warm or has air conditioning, then it is very likely that the interview room will be the same. Given that you cannot change the potential sensory implications of these spaces, it is best to be prepared for and aware of them.

The workplace

Workplaces vary greatly in terms of their potential sensory implications. For example, construction sites contain a very different set of sensory implications to an office. We will begin by looking at the potential sensory issues in an office. It is best to apply the same principles to getting to the office as to getting to a job interview as outlined before. This means that if it is a newly acquired job there should be pre-planning and preparation around how to get there, appropriate clothing, etc. Office spaces may contain a variety of sensory distractions such as the hum of fluorescent lighting, air conditioning, computers or other office equipment.

It may also include phones ringing, people talking or tannoy systems. In many offices work stations are placed very close to each other. It will usually be a requirement of office work that employees will need to interact with each other, and/or collaborate with each other on work projects. There will also be an expectation of interaction during lunch times and break times. Workplaces often have a canteen/restaurant area where people generally congregate for lunch and breaks. These spaces will often be lit by fluorescent lighting and be noisy or have echoes due to their physical structure. This can often be an intimidating or overwhelming space for many people with sensory issues. It is common for people with ASD and sensory issues to find break times and lunch times the most difficult aspect of their working day. This is because of the physical environment as described above, but also because of the social expectation inherent in these spaces.

This expectation can create anxiety for people with ASD who find social interaction difficult, and this in turn may exacerbate their sensory issues. Alternately, the sensory implications of these spaces may be overwhelming and therefore create much anxiety for the person with ASD and make it difficult for them to interact in these spaces.

Other workplaces will bring their own sensory implications as stated at the beginning of this section. Factory work can have bright lighting, strong smells, noisy machinery or equipment as well as having workstations in close proximity (especially assembly line type factory work). Factories may also have canteen or restaurant areas that contain all the sensory difficulties outlined in relation to office dining areas. Construction work will usually involve the use of noisy machinery or equipment as well as bright lights/welding arcs or sparks and a variety of smells.

Though these are just a sample of workplaces one may be employed in, there are usually common sensory features contained within them, particularly in terms of eating areas. Later in this chapter we will look at the creation of a sensory plan for the workplace as part of our overall Sensory Strategy.

Creating a Sensory Strategy

In order to address the variety of ways in which sensory issues may impinge on the lives of people with ASD it is imperative to create a Sensory Strategy. This strategy should encompass all the areas in which sensory issues impinge on a person's life, from travel to shopping, from sex to college and work. Throughout the following chapters we will discuss the different areas of a person's life that may be affected by sensory issues and the methods people may use to address them. All of these taken together can be used to create a Sensory Strategy which will serve as a blueprint to work from, tailor and individualise to address people's own specific sensory needs.

Strategies for managing public and social spaces

There are some common strategies that may be applied which may help alleviate some of the sensory difficulties associated with different public spaces and travel. We will begin by looking at pubs and clubs.

Pubs, clubs and other social spaces

Socialising is an important facet of human nature though the degree of importance to which we individually assign it varies. Some people reach their social fill with relatively minimal contact with others, while other people need to socialise very frequently to reach their social fill. Therefore the amount of time someone may want to spend in a pub is very much dependent on each individual.

However, if someone with sensory issues does want to go to the pub there are ways of minimising the potential difficulties inherent in this space.

The ability to minimise the sensory distractions may be predicated on the ability of the person with sensory issues to become the 'organiser'. This does not mean taking control or taking over the social decisions of the group in a militaristic way! It means offering to contact people with suggestions of pubs to meet in. This then allows the person with sensory issues to pick and choose the pubs that are least likely to cause sensory difficulties. The first method to minimise the sensory difficulties associated with particular spaces is to time visits to the pub to coincide with less busy times. This may be difficult to negotiate with a group but is worth suggesting. The second method is to try to choose pubs that have fewer sensory distractions. For example, a pub that is generally geared towards conversation tends to be more comfortable for people with sensory issues than one with loud music. The third method is to find a space within a pub that is most sensorily comfortable – in other words, a part of the pub away from sensory distractions. This may be an alcove, for example, which is somewhat shielded from the sensory distractions; in this instance it may work best to arrive early and scout the pub looking for the area that is most comfortable for you. The principle of finding a space that is more comfortable in a pub may extend to outdoors – in other words, finding a pub with an outdoor seating area or a beer garden which may be more spacious, comfortable and have fewer sensory distractions.

It is quite difficult to negotiate or mediate against the sensory environment of a nightclub. There are some methods by which to do so. One method would be to have some discreet ear plugs that fit into the ear and are not obvious to others. This will serve to drown out the noise of the music.

It may also create difficulties in maintaining conversations but it is always an option to suggest stepping into a quieter area or outside in order to maintain or continue a conversation. Another method is to try to manoeuvre friends towards clubs that are more sensorily friendly to you. For instance, clubs with a less problematic light show, with less raucous music or with music that has a beat and rhythm that is pleasing to you (this is an issue that many people with ASD identify with. All interviewees for this book said that they prefer the beats/rhythms in certain types of music. As an example, all agreed they did not enjoy the discordant and random element of jazz, while all did enjoy the mathematical and linear progressions of classical and/or pop music. This is not to say everyone with ASD likes only pop or classical, rather it is an expression of preference for certain rhythms within music.) Another possibility is choosing outdoor clubs – similarly to beer gardens they may offer fewer sensory difficulties.

A further option in terms of managing these sensory spaces is to discuss the sensory difficulties with friends. This may be a delicate subject as it depends on how well you know these friends and how understanding they may be, as well as the fact that many people may not feel comfortable disclosing their ASD to others.

An obvious alternative to all of the above is that the person with sensory issues finds a different method of socialising rather than the pub. I made some suggestions earlier as regards the social potential of clubs and societies in colleges but there are many such options for people who are not in college with most towns and cities having a variety of social outlets from sports to activities.

Supermarkets and streets

Some similar methods can be used to mediate against the sensory issues in public spaces and streets as in social spaces. The supermarket can be a place that causes sensory disruption as discussed previously. A holistic way of addressing the sensory issues inherent in supermarkets is to create a sensory plan for it as part of an overall Sensory Strategy. This plan would begin with:

- Writing a shopping list which means greater efficiency, less time spent in the supermarket and less opportunity for anxiety to take hold.

- Use noise-cancelling headphones/Bluetooth headphones to negotiate the cacophony of noises contained in a supermarket or on busy streets.

- Go to the supermarket at quieter/less busy times, such as weekdays, weekday nights. Alternatively use the supermarket at quieter times of the day if possible such as weekday mornings.

- Avoid Friday evening shopping if possible. This principle also applies to streets.

- Keep an eye out for sensory friendly times in supermarkets which have begun to get more common as awareness of sensory issues grows.

Travel

For most people with sensory issues it is inevitable that they will be exposed to environments or situations containing sensory difficulties. This is due to necessity but it is also good practice for people to put themselves into these scenarios as the more exposure to these sensorily difficult situations, the more opportunity the person has to address or overcome them. Also, the more people avoid situations that may create discomfort, the more limited their lives become. Therefore a positive and pro-active approach to these difficulties can be very beneficial and this should be the starting point in the creation of the Sensory Strategy.

In creating the Sensory Strategy it is often worthwhile doing some pre-planning in terms of using transport. For instance, familiarising oneself with the journey on Google Earth, or going on the journey at a quiet time first in order to familiarise oneself with the bus/train, etc. as well as the stops, when and how to get off, does the vehicle stop or do you need to ring the bell. If travelling by plane, familiarise yourself with the airport, how to get to the airport, what documents you need to travel and are they up to date. The use of the pre-planning and relaxation routine (as discussed here) should serve to take much of the anxiety out of these trips and also minimise the sensory difficulties associated with it.

A relaxation routine

Some practical methods that may be useful in terms of managing the potential sensory issues associated with travel include:

- Using headphones/Bluetooth to cancel out noises associated with buses, trains, airports, for example.

- If on a bus, use a time when the bus is less busy where possible.

- Wear clothing that may 'protect' against uncomfortable tactile experiences with other passengers, for example wearing long-sleeved tops. (Interviewee B describes wearing these types of clothes as a way of preventing the discomfort of people brushing against him. He talks about finding 'skin on skin' contact particularly uncomfortable.)

- If flying, try to book flights at less busy times, and/or try to prebook seats at emergency exits as these seats usually have more room (leg room).

If none of the above help or are possible, look at the possibility of using alternative methods of transport. For instance, is it possible to cycle or walk rather than using the bus, or are there train services that can be used as an alternative to the bus?

Also as part of the Sensory Strategy it may be very useful to develop a *relaxation routine*. This will vary from person to person based on what works to relax people individually. Develop the relaxation routine before embarking on whatever form of travel that causes anxiety and sensory difficulties, for example, if getting a bus at 9 a.m. spend five to ten minutes prior to leaving your abode going through your relaxation routine. Some suggestions as to how it may work and what could be included are:

- Mindfulness or meditation.

- Yoga, Pilates, or other forms of physical release.

- Exercises designed to meet individual sensory needs (this is best done by getting an Occupational Therapy assessment), such as chewing gum, feeling certain fabrics, using a trampoline, running or jogging on the spot.

- Many people find the use of relaxing music to be very beneficial.

- Visualisation, i.e. visualising the impending journey and how the person will get through it. (Be aware that this method will work for some and be problematic for others as it may 'promote' procrastination or over-thinking the impending journey to the point that the person becomes more anxious about it rather than less anxious. The point here is to create a routine that will work for each person individually; sometimes that will involve trial and error in finding the right routine for you.)

Work

Given there are a huge variety of different work environments, it is important to create a Sensory Plan blueprint that will be useful across the different work environments. The first potential step in creating a Sensory Plan for the workplace should be looking at the type of work each person is best suited to and whether they are able to manage the potential sensory aspects of the workplace environment. This does not necessarily mean being limited to a narrow range of jobs/workplaces, but it does mean being pragmatic. For example, if a person is particularly sensitive to loud noises then noisy factories or construction sites may not be the best work environment (though there is usually safety equipment provided in most workplaces to prevent hearing damage).

Taking all of this into consideration, it will in most instances be very difficult to find a workplace that does not have some potential sensory components to it. Given that this is likely to be the case, it is best to have a plan as to how to manage any potential sensory difficulties the workplace creates for each person individually. A fundamental and very important issue at this juncture is whether to disclose autism to an employer or not. This is a personal choice that many people on the autism spectrum struggle with as there may be implications to disclosing or not disclosing. Specifically in terms of potential sensory issues in the workplace, the advantage of disclosure is the possibility of creating a better sensory environment in conjunction with the employer and this is what we would recommend where possible. This would mean sitting down and negotiating a sensory plan with the employer, incorporating the following:

- Changing fluorescent lighting or alternatively changing seating arrangements to be a sufficient distance away from the lighting.

- Being given permission to wear headphones or noise-cancelling ear phones where possible. This may be tricky depending on the workplace. Most workplaces will require some degree of interaction with colleagues; therefore the wearing of headphones should not be to the exclusion of communicating with others. It may also bring some questions from colleagues but this may be explained through disclosing the sensory issues.

- Creating a workstation that minimises sensory difficulties; this may mean a workstation that is partitioned, or that is strategically placed in a less sensorily difficult location.

- Creating a workstation/workplace that may have necessary sensory inputs attached to it, for example having Velcro stuck to the bottom of a table for tactile inputs, having cushions or balls on which to balance for proprioceptive and vestibular inputs.

Similarly to school and college it is good practice to pre-empt feeling overwhelmed due to sensory issues by taking time to meet your sensory needs before and during work. Before work it is a good idea to use the relaxation routine we have previously discussed as regards travel. This routine can be universally helpful in terms of dealing with anxieties and sensory issues. It should be built into a morning routine that is broken down step by step into its various components, from getting up and getting dressed to taking a few minutes to practise your routine before leaving the house.

However, it is inevitable that some people will feel overwhelmed in the workplace on occasion. There should ideally be a space that they can go for a time out if they are feeling sensorily overwhelmed. This does not have to be a room specifically set aside, nor does the person need to stand out from their colleagues when using it. This space can be outside, it can be in a different office, a different part of the building or any space that is quiet and allows the person to return to homeostasis (equilibrium). This could be agreed with the manager/supervisor and could take the form of, for example, five minutes per hour on the basis that the employee with sensory needs will be much more productive using this method.

CHAPTER 6

Private Spaces and the Home

The home is generally encapsulated in a permanent physical structure. However, within the boundaries of this physical structure are fluid experiences and meanings of its inner spaces. For example, families come and go through the house and different family members may occupy the house in different ways at different times.

Despite the fact that homes have become 'complex spaces of everyday life' (Crooks 2010, p.45) this primal conception of home remains valid in many ways in contemporary times. It is still seen by many as a space of shelter and safety. For many of those on the AS it provides shelter from a society that may be confusing, intolerant or lacking understanding. Home represents an opportunity to escape from public expectations and the pressure to behave 'normally'. Its physical contours encapsulate an emotional world which is more familiar, with rules that are more easily understood. For a number of the interviewees home represents a place of safety, comfort and protection.

For many people with ASD the control of their environment is a way of minimising potential difficulties, stresses and anxieties. If the space is one in which they control who enters, the sensory inputs, and how the space is physically laid out, then the space becomes much less fraught for them. The adherence to routine and ritual is a core feature of ASD for many (Dubin 2009). The control over a space allows for the person with autism to have a routine that suits their needs. Control over a space may also serve as a counterpoint to the anxieties felt in situations where the rules, expectations and behaviours of and by others is unclear and confusing. The home serves as the primary example of a space that people on the AS may control.

There are several aspects of a given space that may make it bearable or unbearable for many people with autism. These may include, for example, new people that the person with AS may not have met before, or possibly loud noises or pungent smells which may create sensory difficulties (Holliday Willey 1999).

For many with autism, then, it is important that they feel a sense of control over the environment or situation that they find themselves in. Interviewee B articulates this view: 'I am most comfortable in situations where I am in control of the environment because nothing is going to happen that is going to be unpredictable to me'. For many with ASD, the place that they would most be in control of is their home.

The sense of being comfortable is linked to his sense of being in charge, where he is self-directing and where he does not have to negotiate the potential complexities of interactive relationships. The spaces he often feels most uncomfortable in by contrast are those which contain people he is not familiar with:

> I would relate it [feeling uncomfortable] to the knowledge of the people…for instance if I was out with someone I didn't know I would feel uncomfortable, if I was out for dinner with someone I did know I would just feel quite…it wouldn't feel too uncomfortable even if it wasn't somewhere I knew.

For Interviewee B, the space itself may not necessarily cause discomfort for him; rather it is the level of familiarity he has with the people in the space that dictates his level of comfort or discomfort. The people who are in a given space may also dictate what is acceptable or unacceptable, normal or abnormal. He is very conscious of this:

> A completely empty space or an environment empty of people wouldn't be uncomfortable at all because it wouldn't matter how you are in that space and there is no one there to perceive you or judge you, as in, it's like shopping on the internet no one can judge you for what you are doing.

The variety of sensory inputs contained in the home are reminiscent of other social or public spaces; the home may contain noises, sights and smells that may be problematic for some people with ASD. The primary difference, as we have just outlined, is the desire or need for many people with ASD to have the home space as a sanctuary or refuge away from the difficulties associated with public or social spaces. It is more likely for this to be possible if the person is living alone and therefore can create a manageable or even pleasant sensory environment. This may not be possible in a shared space however and therefore it may be necessary to find ways of negotiating the space with others in order to make it more manageable for the person with ASD and their families. One of the primary challenges for people with ASD to share their space with others is that the desire to create a more suitable sensory space may cause friction with others sharing the space as they may feel the space is being controlled or they may not feel the sensory architecture, created to suit one person, will suit everyone else.

The creation of a suitable sensory architecture in a shared space will generally be a negotiation. There are some ways of creating a sensory space that will not cause friction with others, as long as it is negotiated out and agreed by all. One of the best ways of creating a positive sensory space is to divide it up temporally. In other words the person with sensory issues has the house to themselves at certain times, possibly during the day-time if others are working, in college or at school. This means that the various sensory implications of others, from loud music to strong aftershave, cooking smells to screaming children, happen in the afternoon or evening, giving the person with ASD time during the morning/day to have as little (or as many) sensory inputs as they wish.

If it is not possible to divide the sensory space temporally, it may be possible to divide the space into different sections. This may mean dividing the home space up into play areas for children, for example, in which children can play without causing sensory difficulties for others while having a sanctuary within the home that can be retreated to if the person with sensory issues needs to take a sensory break. This can be a bedroom, office, garden shed or just an outdoor space.

A house share/apartment share with others who are not family members may bring its own challenges in terms of negotiating a better sensory space. If the person with sensory issues is in a house/apartment share, the 'sanctuary' method may still be useful as nobody else necessarily needs to know why they need to go to their room or outside. It is important for the person with sensory issues to contemplate whether to disclose their ASD or not to their house mates. Similarly to workplaces, there is the inherent risk of lack of understanding (or caring). On the positive side, it may mean that others are very understanding and may be very supportive and helpful in creating a positive sensory environment. If sharing a house with others, it is a good idea to try to have good routines in terms of cleaning, cooking, etc. This will be helpful in terms of creating a good environment in which to negotiate the space with others. In other words if no-one takes responsibility for housework then it is less likely to be a happy household and it is less likely that anyone will be able to negotiate their sensory needs. There may be ways of creating a positive sensory environment that may benefit everyone in the house. For example, if the person with ASD volunteers to cook for others, this is a way of controlling the potential problematic smells from others' cooking. It would also mean being able to cook the foods that the person with sensory issues does not have taste, smell or texture issues with. (This does not mean only cooking one type of food for everyone; it means being able to cook preferred foods for oneself while cooking less preferred foods for others.) Similar principles may apply to cleaning and the use of cleaning products, some of which may cause sensory issues. There may be an opportunity to volunteer to buy the cleaning products (and choose ones that cause less sensory difficulties). This does not mean that because the person has sensory issues that they should become housekeeper, cleaner and cook; rather everyone in the household should contribute but the person with sensory difficulties can have some element of control in a positive way over their sensory environment.

Shared spaces in a relationship

There are more potentially extreme (but nonetheless worth exploring) ways of people with ASD and their partners to accommodate for sensory issues in their relationship. The most obvious example of this is to divide the home space physically between the partners. This may mean having a section of the house each and then a shared area such as the kitchen. Another manifestation of this principle is living in adjoining houses! (This would obviously involve having the money to afford two houses.) A less extreme example that many couples – both ASD and neurotypical – use is to have separate bedrooms. The advantage of this is the ability for both parties to create a sleeping/relaxing space that is most suitable for themselves (which means it may not be suitable for their partners). This may mean that the person with sensory issues uses weighted blankets, has the walls painted a particular colour, may prefer a type of music or music with a particular rhythm, and may need total silence and darkness, none of which may suit their partner.

It is important that having separate bedrooms does not affect the physical or emotional intimacy of the relationship. This means that there may be compensatory measures necessary to replace the intrinsic intimacy of sharing a bed. Some examples of this may include making more time to partake in activities together, such as walking, art classes or cookery classes – or using our earlier examples of sensory inputs such as taking turns to massage, brush hair/wash hair, or shower together. It is also important that sex does not get shelved on the basis that the partners are no longer sharing a bed every night. A percentage of couples who use separate bedrooms will use the separate bedrooms as a way of 'spicing up' their sex lives by incorporating spontaneity into their routines.

Another method of creating a mutually acceptable shared sensory space is through using everyday chores as a way of dividing the space up. This may mean, for example, both partners agreeing that the person with ASD will do the weekly shopping, or will go to the shop on a daily basis to pick up needed provisions. The advantage of this is that it gives both parties the opportunity to have a space to themselves while the other is out; it also has the added advantage of avoiding arguments over either party not doing enough work in the home! This should not become a demand by one person on the other; it should be agreed upon between both. There are other obvious ways of dividing the space up that follow similar principles such as having 'date nights' which each party chooses for alternative weeks (for example, one partner picks a 'date night' at the ballet for one week while the other partner picks a night at the cinema for the next date night). This means being in neutral space away from the home, the spaces picked should be spaces that do not create sensory difficulties, and the activity of going on these 'dates' will generally have the added benefit of fostering closeness and intimacy.

The creation of timetables/visual schedules can be a very useful way of reducing stress, anxiety and friction in the home for people with sensory issues and their partners. This does not mean having a rigid schedule that is adhered to religiously regardless of circumstances or the wishes of others; instead it is a way of harnessing an aspect of autism for many people that may be used for mutual advantage in a relationship.

An example of how the schedule might work would be the following:

- The schedule should be created by both partners together with agreement on its content.

- It can then be displayed prominently in the kitchen, for example.

- It should be updated weekly; for example, on Sunday evening both partners would sit down and create the schedule for the following week.

- The schedule should ideally include chores for each partner, when children need to be taken to/collected from school and by whom (if there are children).

- The schedule should also include leisure time for each partner, individually and together. It is very important that the needs of both partners are included here; it is vital that sensory needs are being met but this should not be to the detriment of the other person or of the relationship.

- It is important however that the schedule should include any sensory inputs necessary. This may mean taking sensory breaks where the person with sensory issues will incorporate their sensory needs into their daily routine; examples of this may include walks, runs, swims, quiet times, skin brushing, etc.

- The schedule may also include a chores list that is divided between both partners on the basis of equity and what each partner prefers doing (or on what each partner hates doing the least!).

The creation of this schedule should ideally allow for spontaneity as well. This can be achieved by having free time and flexibility around the schedule. In other words the schedule should have a positive impact on the shared space, reducing anxiety and addressing the sensory and other needs of both parties. If it is not achieving this on any matrix then it will need to be discussed and adjusted accordingly. As with any new idea to a relationship (and especially for people with ASD – many of whom may not like change), it may take time to find the most mutually beneficial schedule possible.

Parenting children with ASD and sensory differences

Children and adolescents with ASD should ideally get a full Occupational Therapy assessment including a comprehensive assessment of sensory needs as early as possible. From the parents' perspective, there are a number of areas of the sensory lives of children with ASD that may need to be addressed. The first of these is the home space. Children and adolescents with ASD may experience similar sensory issues as adults with ASD in the home. Unlike many adults with autism, however, children and adolescents with autism do not have a choice about where to live, whether to live alone or how to divide up the home space in a way that better suits their sensory needs.

One of the primary issues that may occur for young people with autism is having to share bedrooms with siblings. Often this is not a significant issue in their younger years but it may become more significant as they get older. The sights, sounds and smells associated with sharing a bedroom with others can be difficult for all young people, it is not the sole domain of young people with ASD, therefore the mutual difficulties in sharing can often manifest in tensions between siblings. There are a number of ways that parents can begin to address this issue. Some examples include allowing siblings to have their own bedrooms if possible. If space is at a premium then look at the possibility of an attic/loft conversion or convert a play room into a bedroom. If this is not possible and there is no option but to have siblings in a shared space then it may be worth dividing the bedroom. This can be done through having a line along the floor (imaginary or created by masking tape) that divides one sibling's space from the other. Allied to this the young person with ASD can be encouraged to use ear plugs/headphones to exclude problematic noises and both siblings can be encouraged to personalise their section of the bedroom (within reason – this does not mean allowing free rein to turn either side of the room into an aesthetic nightmare).

In conjunction with the division of space and the use of sensory aids, it may be worth exploring the use of sensory inputs to address the hyper- and hypo-sensitivity needs of the young person with ASD. This may range from using trampolines to various relaxation methods depending on the sensory profile of the young person. As outlined in Chapter 8, many young people with ASD spend more of their leisure time on screen time than neurotypicals. This can have implications for the person with ASD as it will often mean time spent on the computer or gaming will be to the detriment of time spent socialising with others (though young people tend to interact frequently with others online) or with exercising. This can have the twofold effect of isolating the young person from others and thus having an impact on their mental health, and potentially having an impact on their physical health due a sedentary lifestyle which can often be a major contributory factor in obesity. For many young people with ASD the withdrawal into online spaces represents a withdrawal from problematic sensory environments that may be present in schools or in the home space generally. For parents of young people with ASD it is often advisable to have agreed limits on the amount of screen time the young person spends every day. This is best negotiated from the beginning when the young person first gets access to a computer/gaming console. It is very important to encourage the young person to divide their time between screen time and other activities. Many parents and professionals would suggest the use of a visual schedule as a way of dividing this time out. It could mean, for example, that the young person does their homework after school and then gets screen time. If the young person is stressed and/or anxious after school they may need some time to unwind before doing their homework. If this is the case it is probably best to allow an hour of relaxation or sensory stimulation rather than screen time as it is often very difficult for the young person to limit themselves to one hour and it can often become a point of conflict if parents are trying to move them away from screen time to do homework.

What is very useful is for parents to work with their children in broadening the spaces they can manage rather than allowing a shrinkage of those spaces. The shrinkage of the spaces that the young person with autism feels comfortable in can often result in summers off school spent almost exclusively indoors, or even school refusal where the young person is at home all the time and most of that time at home is screen time. The ability of the young person to manage the anxiety and sensory issues in spaces outside the home needs to be assessed and addressed and parents – in conjunction with appropriate professionals if necessary – need to support and encourage their children with ASD to expand and broaden the spaces they interact in rather than allow these spaces to diminish.

In many cases young people with ASD will withdraw from problematic spaces to those which they have a sense of control over. This is not selfishness on their part; rather it is an attempt to manage their sensory environment and to minimise anxiety. The difficulty for others sharing that space such as parents and siblings is that the space may become uncomfortable for them to share with the person who has autism. This may be especially true if the person with autism is trying to control all the sensory aspects of their environment. This is a complex issue and should be addressed on an individual basis through Occupational Therapy assessment as previously suggested and/or through appropriate professional support. However, there are generalised ways that parents can begin to address the issue of the home space being controlled by a young person with ASD. The first and most important way of beginning to address the issue is to understand why it may be happening in the first place and we have outlined the reasons why over the last paragraph. Having gained an understanding as to why the young person may want to control their sensory environment it may be worthwhile examining their school environment and beginning to assess its suitability for their child. For example, is there an understanding of and provision for the young person's sensory needs in the school? Is there a fully equipped sensory room? Does the young person get sensory breaks? Do the teachers understand the child's sensory needs?

The issue of whether the young person's sensory needs are being met in the school is very important as it will obviously influence their ability to manage the school environment and their ability to learn. If these needs are not being met in the school the knock-on effects are that the child may refuse to go to school or they may expend so much energy trying to manage the sensory anxieties associated with the school environment that they may feel the need to control the home space to counteract the difficulties associated with the school space. Therefore it is advisable for parents to look at all the sensory environments the young person with autism interacts with as they will all have an impact on how they manage the home space. If sensory issues in the school are being addressed then there should not be the same need for the person with sensory issues to control the home space. What should take primacy is that the home space is as comfortable a sensory space as possible for both parents/adults with autism, children with autism and their neurotypical partners and siblings.

CHAPTER 7

Intimacy and the Senses

People with heightened anxiety are more likely to have unusual or problematic sensory experiences (Hofmann and Bitran 2007). Given that people with ASD generally have heightened anxiety there is a direct link between ASD, anxiety and sensory differences, particularly in terms of tactility.

Most people with autism will express the desire to be in a relationship though many will find it difficult to meet partners due to anxiety, sensory, social and communication issues. The spaces where people often meet partners are often exclusionary spaces for those with ASD such as pubs and clubs as we have looked at previously. Therefore people with autism are often limited in terms of the possibility of meeting others, though, as we will explore in the next chapter, there are also other ways of meeting people now through dating sites, internet/social forums and groups, for example. In this chapter we will look at the ways in which dating may have sensory implications, the sensory implications of relationships and strategies for dealing with these.

Dating

Dating is seen as being the method by which two people get to know each other with a view to being in a relationship.

Relationships may take the form of purely sexual relationships (this is usually in the form of one-night stands), platonic relationships (friendships) or long-term relationships (with partners or spouses). The purpose of dating for many people is to meet someone with a view to finding out if they are compatible and, if so, if it is possible to have a relationship with them. Most people will approach a date with an open mind, meaning that they are willing to meet with the person and chat with them before making up their minds as to whether they would like to meet with the person again. Dating will begin with a 'first date' where two people will agree a time and venue to meet with each other. The venue is often a café, restaurant or pub, though this is not always the case (people can and will meet in any venue they feel comfortable in or that suits both parties).

For people with ASD, there is a choice as to whether to tell the person they are meeting for a date that they are on the autism spectrum, or not. We would suggest that it is a risk telling someone as it will vary from person to person how they may react to this. There are many factors to take into consideration. For instance, it is worth considering the possibility that the person may get to know and like the person with ASD first (pre-disclosure) and then be more receptive to the disclosure. (We would hope that now and into the future, as more people become aware of autism, the question of whether someone is going to react negatively to the disclosure that someone has autism will become less and less of an issue.) However, there is also the possibility that the other person will react negatively. For example, if the person does not react well to being told that their date is on the AS then it is likely they will not be compatible in the long term. It is also possible they may not know what autism is and may therefore react by pulling away. Sometimes the person may have a version of what autism is that is based on media stories (this is the principle of a little knowledge being a dangerous thing – in other words only having a very narrow perspective on autism that does not include all the potential positives), which may be misrepresentative of people with autism individually or as a community.

A further consideration when embarking on a first date is the choice of location to meet. Sensory issues may play a big part in the decision about where to meet for many people with ASD; however, this does not necessarily have to be an issue for either party. If the person with ASD has already told their date that they are on the Autism Spectrum then it should be relatively straightforward to meet in a space that has fewer sensory implications. If the person with ASD has not disclosed, then they may suggest meeting somewhere more quiet so that they can talk with their date without fear of interruption. This is where the person with ASD will have the opportunity to choose a quiet café or restaurant, or to meet at an off-peak time where there will be less possibility of sensory difficulties. It will be very important to choose a location without lots of background noise, for example, as this is an issue for many people with autism who find it difficult to focus on what is being said to them and instead may tend to only the background din.

This difficulty in focusing on what the date is saying would generally work against making a good first impression on a first date and also may mean not having the opportunity to get to know about the person. (A good rule of thumb on a first date is to ask the person about themselves. This should not just be a string of questions that may appear like an interrogation; rather it should show the other party that the person with autism is interested in them.) It may be a good idea to visit the location for the first date prior to meeting. This will give the person with ASD the opportunity to acquaint themselves with the space (this may be especially true if the other person chooses the location for the date), choose the least sensorily problematic area, decide where the least problematic acoustics are, whether there is background music, how loud it is in the location generally, what is on the menu, how much money to bring and, if the date goes well, how late it stays open or whether there are appropriate venues nearby that would be suitable to bring a date to after it closes.

Online dating

Online dating offers the opportunity to meet others online mainly. This may mean joining dating sites or may mean meeting others online through specific interest groups or online forums, for example. The advantage of dating sites for people with ASD is the opportunity to look at people's profiles to find people that are interested in the same things. A further potential advantage of using a dating site is that the person can disclose their ASD if they wish and in this way cut out those who may have prejudice or stigmatise autism, while conversely allowing people who understand autism to contact the person with ASD.

The other advantage of using the internet to meet potential partners is that in some instances it offers the possibility of corresponding with others initially as a way of getting to know them before meeting them. This means that there is already a dialogue struck up and this may assist in reducing the anxiety of the person with ASD as they may already have some topics of conversation to turn to when meeting the person face to face. Corresponding online also provides the opportunity to edit and think carefully about what is being written. Furthermore it also allows the person with ASD time to process what is being written to them as opposed to face-to-face communication which can often be difficult to fully process in the moment, particularly if anxiety or sensory issues are impinging on the person's ability to do so. Many people on the autism spectrum find that they are better able to express themselves and articulate who they are through the medium of writing and this can fit in with the initial stages of online dating. It should be noted from the outset, however, that people will have to meet face to face eventually and this is often where people with ASD find that others, who may have seemed interested previously, lose interest having met up. This is usually because the person with ASD is not able to express themselves in the same way when they meet as when they were corresponding online due to anxiety and sensory issues. There are no simple solutions to this but it is advisable to follow the same rules as meeting people in any dating scenario (as outlined in the previous section, pick the location, time, etc., if possible) as a way of minimising anxiety and sensory issues.

Some people would also suggest having topics in mind to discuss when meeting the person for the first time face-to-face for a date. This does not mean scripting – having an entire conversation mapped out before meeting the person. (Scripting is a common method used by people with ASD to deal with social situations that may cause anxiety. It means creating a conversation from one's own perspective, sometimes including expected responses from others, sometimes only including one's own conversation. It is often inspired by theway people interact with each other on film or in TV and hence is quite like an actual script.) The difficulty with scripting is that the conversation almost never follows the form that the person with ASD has created in their own minds. Part of the intrinsic challenge of social interaction for many people with ASD is the unpredictability or variance of conversation with others. Scripting does not answer this problem and it often creates more issues as when the conversation deviates from the ASD person's script they can often become more anxious and disorientated from what is being said. However, there are ways of using some of the principles of scripting in a way that is more helpful for conversation. This means having some general topics in mind to discuss with the person during the date. For example, if the person has mentioned through correspondence or in their profile that they really enjoy classical music then this is a possible topic of conversation. If the ASD person does not share their love of classical music they can still ask the person about their favourite composer or piece. It is generally no harm to know a little bit about the topic if possible, but it is not a good idea to deliver an oral thesis on the best or worst pieces of classical music, rather to ask some questions and show an interest. Usually when embarking on a date it will be because of some shared interests. This is also a good topic to start with on a date; however, it is advisable not to base the entire conversation solely on one particular topic. Try to allow the conversation to move between topics or onto another topic.

Safety

It would be remiss if we did not discuss the importance of safety in terms of online dating and dating generally. There are some fundamental rules that should be followed to ensure safely meeting with others through online dating.[1]

The first is to let trusted others know where you are going (the location of the date) and what time you are meeting the

---

1   Roth and Gillis (2014) discuss Brown-Lavoie *et al.*'s (2014) findings that adults with ASD were three times more likely to experience unwanted sexual contact, 2.7 times more likely to experience sexual coercion and 2.4 times more likely to experience rape than a comparison group.

other person. Trusted others would include parents, family and friends.

You should let others know the name of the person you are meeting for the date as it appears on their profile.

It is not a good idea on the first date in particular to give the person your home address.

It is not a good idea generally to go back to a stranger's place or to a hotel with them. If you do decide to do this then ring or text your trusted others to let them know where you are going and with whom.

Safety is an issue for everyone involved in dating of any kind. In this regard it is vital that both parties' boundaries are respected. This means that if one party says that they are not interested in the other then it is best to move on and find others who may be interested.

Relationship safety in adolescence

The issue of safety in relationships for people with ASD is not just reserved to online dating or dating generally; it also includes safety in terms of the relationships people with ASD may get into in their adolescence. This means that it is important for people with ASD to be aware of their own safety and the safety of others from a young age. For example, it is common for young women with ASD to feel pressurised into sexual relations before they are necessarily comfortable with doing so, or before they have the emotional wherewithal to deal with being in a sexual relationship. The reasons for feeling this pressure may vary from wanting to fit in with peers (the idea that 'all the girls are doing it') to being socially naive towards what potential partners are telling them (for example, potential partners telling the person with ASD that they love them and this is how you express love). In reality it is very important for young people with ASD to have sex education that is targeted specifically for people with ASD. A proportion of schools do not provide adequate sex education and certainly do not provide specialised sex education for people with ASD. It is vital that young people with ASD do not feel pressurised into sexual interactions before they are ready to or before they are able to make an informed and considered decision around doing so. An integral part of sex education for people with ASD should also include dealing with the issue of consent, both the giving of consent for sexual activity and the receiving of consent from potential partners.

It would also be remiss of us to discuss sexual interactions without touching on the area of pornography. The prevalence and easy access to pornography on home computers, laptops and other electronic devices has had a major influence on how young people 'learn' about sex. Combined with the lack of comprehensive sex education in schools and the reluctance or discomfort of many parents to provide sex education, many young people turn to pornography as a way of learning about sex. This may be especially true for people with ASD whose average levels of screen time are higher than neurotypicals. Allied to this, many people do not have as many peer interactions as neurotypicals due to their social communication difficulties and therefore often do not get the opportunity to discuss sexual issues with peers as a way of learning. There are many issues that may be associated with learning about sex through watching pornography, beginning with the misogynistic way in which most pornography is depicted. It is generally aimed at a male audience and tends to portray women as willing participants in male 'fantasy'. It also serves to remove any emotional components from sexual relationships, rather portraying them as a series of sexual acts. This sets a damaging precedence for what a sexual relationship should be for those who look at pornography as a way of understanding the dynamics of a sexual relationship.

In summary, it is vital for young people with autism to have specific sex education (we recommend the work of Isabelle Henault (2006) as an excellent practical way of providing this education).

Sex and sensory differences

It has historically been assumed that people with ASD are often asexual. This has arisen due to the fact that many people with ASD have suggested a lack of interest in being in a relationship, particularly a sexual relationship. However, it is very often the case that when people with ASD discuss in more detail their reasoning for not wanting to be in a relationship, it is because of not understanding social/communication or sexual rules and therefore avoiding the possibility of having to try to understand them in the context of a relationship. We will begin this section by looking specifically at the ways in which sensory issues may play a part in how people with ASD express themselves sexually.

Sex and the senses

Sex is intrinsically a sensory act.[2] It involves sight, smell, taste, touch and sound. It often involves sharing bodily fluids and the very close interaction of bodies against each other. For this reason it can be a potentially extremely pleasant or unpleasant experience for someone with ASD and sensory issues. In order

---

2   Let's take the example of women from Naomi Wolf's book *Vagina: A New Biography*: 'The autonomic nervous system prepares the way for the neural impulses that will travel from vagina, clitoris and labia to the brain, and this fascinating system regulates a woman's responses to the relaxation and stimulation provided by "the Goddess Array", the set of behaviours a lover uses to arouse his or her partner' (2012, p.30).

for sex to be a rewarding experience, the person with ASD needs to be able to discuss with their partner what it is they find pleasant or unpleasant. Central to any relationship therefore is communication. Given communication is often difficult for people with ASD this then presents a challenge in terms of having a rewarding and successful relationship or sexual relationship. The starting point is often about experimenting with what feels good and what does not feel good. This need not be a sterile exercise; rather it can be fun if looked at as an adventure exploring one's own and others' bodies. We would suggest that this experimentation should begin with touch. This involves each person finding out where they like to be touched, where their partner likes to be touched and how much pressure is pleasant or unpleasant, which parts of the body does each person like to be touched with; if it is the hands then is it better for the person to use massage oils, for example. In terms of where a person with autism prefers to be touched, and where their partner prefers to be touched, this tends to be trial and error. For instance, some women do not like to have their breasts or nipples touched, while some men do not like to have their testicles touched. For people with ASD and sensory issues there may be implications of the strength of touch; for example, some people may prefer a lighter touch on some parts of their bodies while a heavier touch on other parts. The important part about this experiment is communicating clearly with partners to tell them what works best for oneself, and also finding out from partners what works best for them. This may also involve a compromise as the things each of us individually like doing may not be what our partner prefers and vice versa. It is vital that this is respected on both sides. While it is okay to compromise and do some things that please a partner even if they may not be our favourite thing to do, it is also important that our wishes and theirs are ultimately respected as feeling obliged or forced into doing something that we/they do not want to do can be very harmful; therefore consent must be sought in all situations.

In terms of creating a suitable setting for a sexual encounter it is very important to take the environment into consideration. This means having a suitable location where both parties are comfortable with their surroundings. We would not generally recommend experimenting with each other in a public place for the first time; it may be best to begin getting to know each other sexually in a more private and comfortable space before considering moving the location of our sexual interactions. For most people this means beginning in the bedroom. In order for this to be a comfortable experience the sensory environment should be suitable for both parties. This means a suitable temperature for the room, with no unpleasant aromas, off-putting sounds, lack of privacy, unsuitable lighting, unsuitable texture or patterns to bedding/mattresses, walls, etc.

What can often be useful in terms of knowing what will work sexually with a partner is knowing one's own body. This means knowing what may be pleasant or unpleasant for us through self-exploration. The most common method of sexual self-exploration is through masturbation. Masturbation serves to inform us as to what feels good to us, what pressures, body parts, sex toys (e.g. vibrators), sensations and rhythms are most pleasurable for us. For most people masturbation is a way of achieving orgasm and it is often the case that we become the experts on what works best for us to achieve that goal. This can be really helpful as well in terms of discussing with a partner what we like and what works for us. If we can guide our partner to the ways that work best for us then this can be a way of reaching orgasm.[3] Though there is little research on the subject of ASD, sensory issues and orgasm, there is anecdotal evidence of heightened sensations for some people that make either reaching orgasm easier than most people without sensory issues, that the orgasm itself is experienced in a heightened way (this is very difficult to measure as each person experiences their orgasm subjectively and also each time orgasm is reached is different) or that it is very difficult to reach orgasm due to anxiety, or sensory hypo-sensitivity that affects the ability of the person to reach orgasm. In terms of sensory tactile sensations generally, Interviewee B discusses his over-arousal in situations where it may not be appropriate to become aroused such as when hugging friends. His sensory tactile system is heightened to any touch that involves pressure and this can be quite common amongst people with ASD. For example, many people with ASD will talk about only achieving orgasm where they experience deep pressure on their entire body. Others with ASD and sensory issues will need specific pressure on particular body parts in order to achieve orgasm. An example of this may be where some people will need extra pressure around their penis in order to achieve climax.

An integral part of sex for most people is spontaneity. This means being able to spontaneously have sex or sex acts when both people feel suitably aroused and motivated to do so. For many people with ASD spontaneity represents lack of control and can often be a scary proposition. The strict adherence to a routine can be a way of controlling the many variables including spontaneity that can be problematic for

---

3   From the outset we should make it clear that sexual satisfaction is not predicated on the ability of either or both partners to reach orgasm. The likelihood is that the more pressure each partner feels to have an orgasm, the less likely it is to happen. Also the pursuit of orgasm can often lead to staid or mechanical sex rather than spontaneous or organic sex.

people with autism. Routine represents certainty and this will usually have the effect of easing anxiety and controlling sensory issues. Routine can therefore be a source of comfort in a world that can often feel fluid, uncertain and filled with potential stumbling blocks. The difficulty with routine in terms of a sexual relationship is that both parties are unlikely to want to stick with the same routine interminably. For instance, having sex at certain times, on certain days and only in certain positions can be problematic if both parties are not as invested in the routine. This also serves to remove the possibility of spontaneity from sexual encounters and may lead to one or possibly both parties becoming dissatisfied. An important point to take into consideration in this regard is that even if a particular day, time or sexual position worked for both parties at the beginning of a relationship, for example, this does not necessarily mean it is the only way for people to have sex, or that it should continue throughout a relationship. The most successful sexual relationships tend to be ones where spontaneity, excitement, experimentation, compromise, communication, safety and consent are present. Of the important components that make up a successful sexual relationship communication is the key. This means both parties being able to discuss their desires and needs openly with each other. It also means being able to move beyond the rigidity of set routines which may prove detrimental to the relationship.

Fantasy often plays a part in the sex lives of people. This can stretch from fantasising during sex to dressing up or fetishistic behaviour. For people with ASD and sensory issues the use of fantasy can potentially be problematic if it involves the use of props that may be sensorily uncomfortable. The primary starting point with the introduction of any type of fantasy/ fetishistic behaviour is communication and consent. Viewing the use of fantasy from a positive perspective, people with autism and sensory issues who may enjoy the sensation of certain types of materials may derive sensory pleasure from wearing certain types of clothing which it may be possible to introduce into sexual or physical encounters (this may include people who are only able to achieve orgasm when they have contact with certain materials or textures). Some people may enjoy certain fetishes; for example, some may focus on certain body parts in particular (known as partialism) and this could be incorporated into sex. The key point here is that any fantasy or fetishistic behaviour should be discussed in advance and consent agreed between sexual partners. Used in an open and playful way, fantasy and fetish can serve to increase the enjoyment of sexual partners while also potentially meeting the sensory needs of a person with ASD and sensory issues.

A more general way of incorporating a person's sensory differences into a relationship is to use the sensory inputs that are pleasurable as a way of increasing the satisfaction of both partners. This means taking the everyday sensory stimuli that the person with sensory differences experiences and using them during intimacy or during sexual activity. For example:

- Particular music/songs can be stimulating or relaxing.
- The smell of oils, scented candles or sex liniments may be pleasant.
- The feeling of very hot hot or very cold water can be stimulating.

The person with sensory differences can explore the inputs in their daily lives that are pleasant and incorporate them into their relationship. This does not have to mean that they are incorporated into their sex lives only; rather that they can be incorporated into the relationship generally. This may mean using certain sensory inputs as part of foreplay or simply as part of making one's partner or oneself feel good. Many couples will use massage, for example, as a form of foreplay or just as a pleasant intimate experience and pleasant sensory inputs can have the same effect for people with sensory differences. What is important here is for the person with sensory differences to take note of what feels good in their daily lives (this may mean writing it down somewhere secure from others' prying eyes) and then discuss it with their partner and use the inputs in their relationship. Some examples of this may be incorporating the sensation of enjoying rain on the skin by having a cold shower before becoming intimate (if both parties are brave enough they could share the shower!). Another example of a sensory stimulatory act that could be mutually enjoyable is the brushing of skin with a hand brush. Through communication it may be possible to find ways of using the brush that is most pleasant for the person seeking sensory stimulation. This may mean brushing in straight lines or brushing in circles – depending on what is most pleasant for the recipient. Both of these methods may be especially useful to someone who is hypo-sensitive but it is also important to meet the hyper-sensitivity needs that someone with ASD may have. This may mean, for instance, listening to music that the person finds relaxing and soothing. Another example may be lying in a darkened room with a minimum of sounds or any other sensory inputs.

Relationships and intimacy

One of the primary building blocks of good relationships is intimacy. This does not necessarily mean physical or sexual intimacy; it can also mean emotional intimacy. Many people with autism find emotional intimacy a difficult proposition but with communication and practice a way of expressing intimacy can often be found. This may mean using our example above of the shower as a way of fulfilling a sensory need or it may mean partaking in an activity together that one or both partners enjoy, for example running together, boardgames or hillwalking. If possible it is a useful bonding exercise for both partners to be able to participate together as it promotes intimacy and bonding and is thought to stimulate oxytocin release which is a neurochemical implicated in the bonding process.

Communication

As we have made clear throughout this chapter, a further fundamental building block to any successful relationship is communication. In most relationships regardless of whether either or both of the partners have ASD, issues with communication are often the root cause of difficulties. In relationships where one or both partners have ASD then it is often even more important. Given that difficulties with communication are very frequent for people with autism, it is vital that methods of communication are found that allow both partners to express themselves. This may mean using written communication if necessary. An example of this may be using a diary that is shared between both partners as a way of expressing needs, desires, intimacy or any other communications to do with the relationship that should be shared. This does not mean using the diary to berate partners for not doing the dishes or cleaning the fridge; it should be specifically used as an instrument of communication to express or articulate issues of intimacy between the partners in the relationship. A practical example of how this may be used is where a person with sensory needs writes what sensory inputs they may need in order to promote intimacy or to get them in the right frame of mind for having sex. It may not always be easy for a person with ASD to be able to articulate that verbally and this may mean that the issue never gets aired and remains as an unspoken difficulty. This diary should be kept in a private place where only both partners have access.

A further method of tailoring communication to suit people with ASD who may have difficulties expressing themselves verbally is to look at methods that take sensory issues into account and adjust the expectations of what neurotypicals may expect of 'normal' communication. For instance, many neurotypicals will say that their ASD partner does not listen if they are criticising them. Oftentimes this can be because of anxiety, an inability to process what is being said if it is being said too quickly, a difficulty processing words that are being shouted at them because the volume is uncomfortable, difficulty understanding the emotions of the other person, or not necessarily understanding why they are angry. What may be useful in this scenario is for the person who is upset to write down in unemotional language why they are upset and give this to their partner. If they have become spontaneously upset it may be possible to write the reasons down in the moment so it may be worthwhile saying what they feel needs to be said then allowing the person with ASD to process this (as opposed to continuing to 'make' the person understand which may prove counterproductive). From the perspective of the person with sensory issues it may be worthwhile exploring methods of being able to listen to what is being said to them by minimising other sensory inputs. This may mean, for example, being in a darkened room while the other person talks to them. In this way the person with sensory issues is reducing the other sensory distractions that may be affecting their ability to take in what their partner is saying to them (in most homes there are a variety of distractions such as children, cooking or television/radio/laptop).

Children

In many cases people in long-term relationships will decide to have children together. This does not mean that people who are in long-term relationships or marriages must have children; it just means that many choose to have children. Having children inevitably changes the nature of a relationship. It changes the emotional architecture of the home environment but children also bring many new sensory components to the lives of people with sensory differences. The first way in which these new sensory components may manifest begins for women with pregnancy. Pregnancy obviously changes the female body and mind physically, chemically and emotionally. This invariably changes the sensory world of the pregnant woman also; their body looks and feels different. As the gestation period evolves so the weight equilibrium in the body changes and this may have an effect on the vestibular and proprioceptive systems of the person. There is no way of avoiding this change obviously but rather to be aware that these physical changes will happen and to manage the potential sensory implications involved.

Further changes may occur in the body such as nausea (frequently referred to as morning sickness though it does not necessarily only happen in the morning), developing desires to eat particular foods that may not have previously been desirable, or being unable to tolerate the taste or smell of foods that may not previously have been an issue. It is very important to seek advice from a GP, paediatrician or other relevant medical expert in terms of maintaining a suitable diet throughout the pregnancy. This is especially important if, for example, the mother-to-be already has a limited diet due to sensory-textural or taste issues around food. It is about finding the right diet that takes into consideration sensory and pregnancy needs while also providing sufficient healthy nutrition for mother and baby (if necessary it may be worthwhile consulting a reputable dietician/nutritionist).

Childbirth may also involve a variety of sensory issues for expectant mothers. This includes the sights, sounds and smells of the hospital environment but also includes the act of childbirth itself. This will usually involve the use of medication through an IV (intravenous) line which will be inserted into the mother's arm; this may or may not create sensory issues as most mothers at this point will welcome pain relief. However, many (though by no means all) mothers with ASD and sensory issues may enjoy the feelings associated with childbirth including the pain involved. The best way to prepare for this experience is to discuss the entire procedure with the relevant medical staff well in advance of giving birth so there are no surprises on the day. Another useful strategy is for the mother-to-be and their partner to familiarise themselves with the hospital environment and take note of the sensory inputs present. This obviously means being forewarned and therefore gives both partners the opportunity to take steps which may make the experience less sensorily difficult. For example, if the smells of the hospital are problematic then it may be possible to mitigate against this by the mother-to-be having a handkerchief with a relaxing scent on it in her hand and placing it under her nostrils when required (or her partner could do this for her if necessary). If the sounds of the hospital create a difficulty then it may be useful to have headphones at hand to be put on as required or alternatively having discreet in-ear ear plugs (please note that when using ear plugs make sure the mother-to-be and her partner are able to hear the instructions from the medical staff!).

When a child is born it brings with it a new set of sensory components that may be pleasant and unpleasant for parents with ASD (as well as neurotypical parents) and sensory differences. Some parents with ASD find the smell of babies to be pleasant and often seek it out; others will find the variety of smells associated with babies to be unpleasant. What may be helpful in terms of the smells associated with babies is to choose baby-friendly washing powders, soaps and shampoos that do not cause sensory difficulties. This should ideally be done before the baby is born and may require some trial and error with different products to find what is best suited. The same principle will apply to the baby's clothing and bedding. Both parents are going to be interacting very frequently with the baby and therefore consideration should be given to the textures the baby is swathed in. These textures need to be pleasant to both the parents and the baby. Again it is best to experiment with the textures before the baby is born to ensure suitable clothing, for example, is found. It is also imperative that in doing so the clothing is suitable for babies and that their bedding meets all fire safety regulations (this should be indicated on the label). The next potential issue may be the food the baby eats. For some parents with sensory issues the thought of touching baby food that might be wet and viscous in texture may be problematic. There are ways of dealing with this such as finding suitable baby foods that may have more pleasant textures or smells. If this is not possible then it may be worthwhile investing in disposable surgical gloves so that the skin does not come in contact with the food.

Bonding with the child is a vital part of the developmental process. An integral part of bonding can be eye contact. This may cause sensory issues for people with ASD who may find eye contact to be too intense, overwhelming or unpleasant. There may not be an easy solution to this issue. Parents should not feel under pressure to make continuous eye contact or to force themselves to make eye contact; however, it is important to make some eye contact and it is best if this happens naturally through the everyday interactions with the baby. If it is not happening due to sensory discomfort then it may be worthwhile for both partners to have a discussion about how best to address it. Sometimes with a little practice over short periods of time it may become manageable.

What is arguably more important is the tactile relationship that is vital to the bonding experience between parents and their children. This may be difficult for people with sensory/tactile issues to deal with. The suggestions we have made previously in terms of clothing and bedding should be very helpful in this regard but if parents are still finding it difficult to manage the tactile sensory implication of handling a baby then it may be worth using some other sensory stimulatory methods either before or after handling the baby which make the experience more manageable. This may mean for example holding a texture that feels very pleasing as a way of getting a pleasant sensory input. (If it is possible to incorporate this texture into the clothing and bedding of the baby then it may be worth doing so; however, babies will need to be bathed, changed, etc.). It is very important that the baby is comforted when crying, if for example they are teething. This takes some practice to create a movement that is soothing for the baby and it may also be soothing for the parents with sensory issues. The act of gently rocking the baby in the parent's arms may be a way of pleasantly stimulating the parent's vestibular system. What is very important in this regard is to recognise the baby's needs, what they are communicating to the parents and how the parents should best respond to this. This takes time and practice and will involve the parents getting to know their children. If the parents have a difficulty recognising what their babies are trying to communicate to them, there are many really useful books and websites that can be drawn on as a resource to learn how to do so.

A final potential sensory issue for parents of babies is the tendency for babies to cry or scream. For parents with sound sensitivity, this can be a difficult issue to negotiate. Given that there is no way of preventing a baby from occasionally crying or screaming, it is up to the parents to develop methods of coping with these sounds. An obvious way of doing so is by using ear plugs but we would urge caution with the use of these. They should only drown out the worst excesses of the noises but should not in any way affect the parent's ability to manage their child's safety. In other words, the parent should still be able to hear the child clearly and the ear plugs should only be used while with the child. An alternative to this is to play soothing music for both parents and babies alike. This can be popular music or lullabies which many adults also find relaxing.

As children grow up they obviously change and begin to bring new sensory inputs with them into the lives of their parents. This means that parents may need to adjust and evolve their responses to these new sensory inputs (though they will generally revolve around similar sensory issues such as smells and sounds). Allied to this will be the expectations attached to each era of the child's life, from the expectation of nurturing and bonding in the early years, to being able to understand the issues teenagers experience in trying to fit and exert their own independence. The sensory needs of parents with ASD are very important in terms of having children; however, it is also very important for parents (neurotypical parents and those with autism) to understand the sensory needs of children and teenagers with autism. We have explored the school/classroom sensory needs of children with ASD in Chapter 4; it is also very important to take into consideration the non-classroom sensory needs of children with ASD.

CHAPTER 8

Cyber Space

The interactive potential of cyber space

Virtual space or cyber space exists both between and in public and private spaces. It is a public space that may be used for social interaction while being accessed from a private space. Cyber space in the form of the internet can provide an alternate space through which people on the AS may interact with each other, and with 'neurotypicals'. It represents a space that is potentially less sensorily stressful, stigmatising, uncomfortable and exclusionary than public spaces (Davidson and Parr 2010). Much research has shown the benefits of the internet for those with ASD (Armstrong 2010). This has included online forums providing help and support for individuals with ASD. It has also facilitated the creation of the neurodiversity movement which began as, and continues to be, an online-based movement. The potential for use of the internet for those with ASD as a space for interactive and educational purposes has been explored by various authors (e.g. Parsons and Mitchell 2002).

However, the homogenous nature of the ASD population dictates that not all on the spectrum use the internet for interaction. Many people with autism express a preference for interacting with others in 'real' space/time: 'Most of us also crave companionship' (Simone 2010, p.95). However, others fear that if they meet friends in actual, as opposed to virtual, space then aspects of their ASD may make it difficult for them to interact comfortably, by setting them apart as 'different'; a proportion of people with autism feel a sense of safety in the virtual space as it is a more forgiving space. For example, the internet allows people time to process conversation. In this way they may not feel under the pressure of real time as they have a couple of minutes to process what they have been told and respond accordingly.

For people with autism the internet may serve as a space for professional use, or for gaming. Interviewee A feels that the internet as a space does not adequately convey all aspects of an interaction: 'I find it difficult to talk to people when they can't hear the tone of my voice, it's more difficult when it's pure text…there's a kind of dimension of communication that's cut off when it's not spoken, for me'. This opinion of the interviewee is contrary to much research posited around ASD and which suggests the inability to read others' thoughts, feelings and emotions, and it serves to show the diversity of the ASD population (Baranek 2002). The interviewee expressed a preference for communication where he could hear the intonations of the voices of those he is communicating with, and that they could hear his. The nuanced nature of his verbal communication is also evidence of the homogenous nature of the ASD community, not all of whom talk in a monotone way, though some do: 'Individuals with ASD often exhibit a constricted range of intonation that is used with little regard to the communicative functioning of the utterance' (Klin, Volkmar and Sparrow 2000, p.323).

Cyber space therefore may serve as a space where some people with ASD are able to control anxieties and fears and communicate with others (which is something that many of those with ASD desire), but for others it is a diminished space which serves to undermine their ability and desire to communicate.

The sensory implications of cyber space

Cyber space represents a space unlike physical spaces in that it can be entered into from wherever there is access to a computer; 98 per cent of young people generally use a computer for on average 4.9 hours (Kuo *et al.* 2014). This means potentially bypassing all of the sensory issues that may be inherent in public or private spaces. This is a relatively complex issue that we will explore in as simple a fashion as possible by creating a binary view of the potential positives and negatives of using cyber space as a means by which to bypass sensory issues.

Positive implications

The positive implications of cyber space as a space in which to interact, relax and game with others begins with the all-pervasive nature of cyber space. This means having the conduit to communicate with others throughout the world from one's own computer and this in turn means having a greater possibility of interacting with like-minded people. This may be especially the case for people with ASD who may not have friends in their locality, or people who may be geographically isolated in rural areas where it is difficult to physically meet up with others. A further potential advantage specifically in terms of sensory issues is that people who find social or public spaces to be sensorily problematic may withdraw from these spaces and therefore limit their possibility of interacting with others in these spaces. Cyber space however represents a space free of sensory difficulties and so allows people to interact with others without having to contend with the difficulties associated with social or public spaces. This means being able to connect with people anywhere in the world individually or through forums and blogs, for instance. As previously stated, cyber space has served as a very significant space for many people with ASD not only to communicate with others but also to represent themselves. For many people with ASD there is less likelihood of having the opportunities to represent themselves in any other space than cyber space because of the platform this space provides and the potential numbers of people it can reach, but also because it allows the person to concentrate on the message they are trying to get across rather than being distracted or disturbed by sensory issues.

Cyber space also offers the opportunity of gaming which, as we will explore, can be both a negative and a positive experience for people with ASD. It presents the possibility of interacting with others in the gaming community which many people with ASD may be missing in their lives generally. A substantial number of people with ASD would say that gaming represents a relaxing alternative to the difficulties encountered in life generally. They may feel that they get their 'fill' of public spaces and their fill of sensory inputs in their daily lives and they use gaming as a counter-balance to this, a space in which there are set rules that can be easily understood, where there are no anxieties about how to interact with others and where they don't need to contend with the sensory implications of other spaces. Many would also feel that it offers an opportunity to be part of a community, an opportunity that may not be available in the rest of their lives generally.

Technology offers a number of ways for people with sensory and social differences to interact with the 'real' world. For many people, it serves as a 'shield' against some of the difficulties associated with certain spaces. For instance, a huge proportion of people now use personal music players of one sort or another in public spaces. These devices can range from phones to tablets (or even phablets). They can be extremely useful in blocking out unnecessary sounds in sensorily stressful spaces as well as providing comfort and familiarity in terms of songs being played. Interviewee F describes using his headphones to help mediate against the difficulties he experiences on busy public streets. He feels without having his headphones on playing songs he finds relaxing (usually the same song on repeat) he would not be able to cope with the demands of being in this space. A further purpose of the headphones in his case, and for many others, is that it allows him to walk through the crowds without the possibility of someone trying to speak with him. In this way the headphones serve to some extent to limit the problematic variables, the unexpected occurrences that make this space a difficult one for him. In some ways the limiting of the possibility of unexpected or unwelcome interactions represents one less thing for him to be anxious about in an environment containing many anxieties. The use of headphones in this way is useful in many similarly problematic public spaces.[1]

This interviewee also discusses the use of his smart phone as a method by which to offset anxieties and sensory difficulties. For example, he talks about feeling anxious when he has to drive somewhere that he is not familiar with, or

---

1   In many ways the prevalence of personal music players which most people use in public spaces or on public transport is a way for people, regardless of being on the AS or not, to shut out their immediate environment and is often used as a way of not having to converse with others. This is representative of a melting away of the perceived differences between people with autism and neurotypicals and creates the platform for a discussion on a different forum as to whether the differences between neurotypicals and people with autism are as defined as is often presumed. I am reminded of the words of Collins who said that autism may be 'an overexpression of the very traits that make our species unique' (Collins 2004, p.161).

has never been to. His anxiety stems from going somewhere new, breaking routines in terms of the route he has become accustomed to and the difficulties being able to listen to Sat Nav and concentrate on his driving simultaneously. The smart phone offers a lifeline to maps, information and being able to call his family if he gets lost or starts to feel overwhelmed. The phone does not have any sensory implications for him in the way that Sat Nav does and it serves to comfort him even if he does not end up using it during his journey.

It is not only headphones or phones that allow people to use technology as a means by which to manage their difficulties in public spaces. For example, many people will use their laptops or tablets in public spaces as a way of creating an individualised private space within a public space. The implications of this for people with sensory differences are similar to those offered by using headphones. It provides comfort and allows for the mitigation of difficult sensory inputs. However, it also allows people to interact virtually with others in a space that is comfortable while being in a space that may be difficult and uncomfortable. This also melts some of the barriers that exist for people with sensory and social differences in public spaces. It allows for social interaction to take place in the public space, just not with the people who are actually in the space. This can also be very comforting and useful as it can distract the person from the difficulties associated with the space but also connect with others who may have similar difficulties. (Sometimes it may be possible for this to happen in real time and for people to connect with each other, interact and describe where they are and what difficulties they may be experiencing – with others who have similar difficulties – while they are actually in the space and experiencing the difficulties.)

Cyber space can also be used as a medium for understanding autism. Given the increasing propensity for people to use the internet to understand medical, psychological, social and neurological issues, it is understandable that many people with autism will use it as a way of understanding autism. We have included this in the positives section around cyber space on the basis that it allows for interactions with others on the AS and in the negatives section for the reasons outlined later.

In terms of the positive implications for understanding, we have previously discussed the use of cyber space as one in which people with autism have created a culture and sense of community. One of the component parts of the creation of that community is based on common understandings. This is true of sensory issues in particular, though given the historic lack of importance attached to the part sensory issues play in the experience of autism for many people, this is a burgeoning area. What cyber space offers specifically in terms of understanding sensory issues is the many boards and blogs where people with ASD will describe their sensory experiences. For people on the AS who have just been diagnosed, are still struggling with understanding what that means or are having difficulties in certain areas of their lives but have not connected it to sensory issues, this sharing of experience can be invaluable. Many people with autism will describe feeling a sense of belonging on the basis of interacting with the stories of others who may have had similar difficulties. Feeling like you are not the only one who feels like they are just about hanging on to their composure when experiencing borderline meltdown in a supermarket can be an extraordinarily validating experience for many who may have previously felt or experienced a lack of understanding from those around them. In this sense cyber space can be used as a vehicle by which to re-appropriate what is deemed as 'normal'. Many people on the AS will share those feelings of sensory anxiety in a supermarket; these feelings that may be deemed as 'abnormal' by those who do not share or understand these experiences. The interaction with others online who share these difficulties has served to re-shape the boundaries of what is 'normal' or 'abnormal'.

Negative implications

Having looked at the many positive implications of cyber space we will now turn to look at the negative implications. The first of these is the potential for people with autism to turn to cyber space in the first instance as being a space that is more comfortable to communicate in as well as being more sensorily comfortable than public or social spaces. This may be problematic in that it may promote the avoidance of social or public spaces as they may contain too many sensory implications. The potential fallout from this may be the diminished ability of the person to interact with public spaces; simply put, the less a person with ASD practises interactions in public spaces, the more difficult they are likely to find it when they inevitably have to engage with the spaces. (Given the inevitability of having to interact in public spaces at some time – in school, college, work, shopping, etc. – the avoidance of public spaces will make each occasion when an individual has to interact in or with these spaces even more difficult.) It also diminishes the impact of any Sensory Strategy as the strategy is based on experiential learning and this learning will usually take place in public or social spaces.

Another potential difficulty of using cyber space is that people who interact on social media for example often send out an avatar, a cyber version of themselves that often is an exaggerated or embellished version that tends to only focus on the person's good points or positive experiences (this is not universal but is very prevalent). There is the further potential for people to 'overshare' their private lives online. By this we mean not having boundaries as to what should be divested through the means of a very public platform.

This is representative of how people interact with the world through cyber space, where they have become increasingly likely to share information on a forum that is public and is accessible by people they do not know, as well as by present or potential future employers (in this sense there is a lack of recognition of the fact that cyber space is never a private space and furthermore all interactions with and on this space are available into the future).

Therefore, though cyber space may provide social potential, it may not always provide a 'realistic' version of people and therefore distort the process of interaction. This may be especially problematic for people on the AS who may have difficulties with social interaction, communication or social cues. This difficulty can often be framed as being a social 'naivety' where the person on the AS is more likely to take others' words literally and to expect them to be truthful. This has the potential to be especially problematic in social media where Facebook and other social media tools are used as a platform by which people generally represent themselves and their lives in a relentlessly positive fashion to the exclusion of the practical and existential difficulties that most people experience. If someone with autism is already struggling to find their place in a neurotypical dominated world, as well as trying to understand their own emotions and the emotions of others, it can cause further confusion if the version of 'normal' behaviour as represented through social media sites is reductive or false.

Furthermore, there is the potential for people to be less empathetic or to be nasty via cyber space. It appears that people are more likely to be nasty via the internet as there is a perceived distance between themselves and the objects of their scorn. (We can see extreme versions of this in the military – for example, the use of drones to destroy targets. The drones are controlled by pilots in a control centre far removed from the actual site where the targets are being struck.) It also appears as if people who do pour scorn on others do not feel the same sense of consequences as those who do it face to face; we have much evidence of these phenomena in the form of cyber bullying. This means that though cyber space does offer a space free of sensory issues there may be many other issues that people with ASD may have to contend with.

This leads us on to the potential for cyber space to be used as a medium for understanding autism. We have included this in the positives section around cyber space on the basis that it allows for interactions with others on the AS. However, we are also including it in the potential negatives section. This is because of the potential negatives around autism on the internet in terms of negative representations of autism (everything from bogus associations between autism and violence to the idea of people with autism being from a different planet, which has serious connotations in terms of the notion of people on the AS as being 'less than human') as well as what we would term the commodification of autism. By this we mean the opportunistic and often cynical selling of 'products' or interventions supposed to assist, support or 'cure'. This can be particularly cynical when it preys on the very real needs and worries of both parents and people with autism themselves and in many ways puts a monetary value on fear and desperation.

Cyber space – the research bit

Cyber space is multi-functional and thus far we have focused on the social potential of the space in terms of communication and interaction. It is also a space in which people participate in activities of relaxation or pleasure such as gaming. Many people with ASD use cyber space to game, and specifically to game with others. (Studies have shown that children with ASD spend on average 4.5 hours per day on screen time. Children with ASD spent 62 per cent more time involved in screen-based activities than non-screen including physical activities and spending time with friends.) This can be a very enjoyable experience as well as one in which the person feels part of a community of sorts. However, it may also bring pitfalls in terms of the potential for people to become overly involved in gaming, or to use gaming as their only social outlet – often to the exclusion of any others. It is common for people with ASD to want to control their own space as we have explored previously; this is often manifest in controlling their internet usage also and can be a particular issue for adolescents with ASD and their families. Some people with ASD will withdraw almost fully into gaming as a space that can be controlled and as a space of fantasy without the potential sensory difficulties that may be experienced in other spaces.

Excessive use of 'screen time' is linked to both poor academic performance and less time spent interacting and in physical activity (Johnson *et al.* 2007; Sharif and Sargent 2006; Sharif *et al.* 2010). There is also increasing evidence of internet usage being an 'addiction'. Video-game play in particular can lead to addictive-like behaviours (increased tolerance, withdrawal, relapse, mood modification – using it to feel better, conflict) (Chou, Condron and Belland 2005; Meerkerk *et al.* 2009). It can mean skipping school to play games, not engaging in social activities and becoming angry when not being able to play (Griffiths and Hunt 1998). This anger/difficult behaviour is more prevalent in boys with ASD than neurotypical children (Mazurek and Wenstrup 2013); 41 per cent of parents reported that their child with ASD aged 13–17 spent most of their free time playing video games (Mazurek *et al.* 2012). Increased use of internet especially video gaming is shown to have an impact on mental health

(Ferguson, Coulson and Barnett 2011). In adults, problematic internet use is associated with loneliness (Morsahan-Martin and Schumacher 2000), depression (Van Den Eijnden *et al.* 2008) and poor relationships (Kerkhof, Finkenauer and Muusses 2011) with mothers and peers (Sanders *et al.* 2000).

Cyber space – a happy medium

Having explored the potential negative and positive implications of cyber space we will now discuss finding a happy medium – where people with ASD can engage with cyber space and use it positively to benefit themselves. The key to finding the happy medium is essentially about striking a balance between using cyber space in ways that can be useful without becoming too immersed in it and without letting it decrease social interactions. Ideally engaging in and with cyber space should be about using its social potential to embellish the social activities people are involved with in their daily lives. An example of this may be using social media to find out about and join groups that reflect a person's own interests – for example, hillwalking, boardgames or cycling.

For most people, meeting with others socially will involve being in social spaces such as those we have described previously – pubs, clubs, cafés, etc. These spaces contain potential sensory difficulties for many people with autism. The benefit of corresponding with friends or potential partners through cyber space is that it removes the sensory component from the interactions and allows the person with ASD to maintain contacts with friends. Looking at this from the opposite perspective, many people with ASD may lose contact with friends if they feel the only way they can maintain the friendship is by meeting in spaces that they find sensorily problematic. This may lead to the person with autism avoiding these spaces and falling out of touch, or meeting in these spaces but finding it very difficult to interact because of sensory issues. This is not to say that it is a good idea for someone with autism to completely avoid social spaces; rather that cyber space in this instance also can serve to promote social contact when used in conjunction with meeting people in social spaces.

Gaming can be a very enjoyable and relaxing experience. It can also be a way of being part of an online community of gamers and thus promoting interaction of sorts (it is a positive that people will interact via gaming but ideally it should not be the only interactions people have in their lives). Gaming also represents a way of being involved in an activity that does not have sensory implications in the way that most activities do – for instance, most sports and many other activities that may be indoor or outdoor. Using cyber space for relaxation and enjoyment through the expression of an interest is generally a positive element of the lives of many people with ASD. However, there is a real danger of people becoming too immersed in the online world as we have explored previously and it is incumbent on each individual to ensure that there is a balance struck between online time and offline time. There are many people with ASD who 'disappear' into the online world and thus blur the lines between reality and fantasy. In many of these cases this will have an impact on family members, partners or others sharing the home space, especially if the person is spending all of their free time online. The implications of spending too much time online also include the possibility of becoming addicted as we pointed to in our 'negatives' section. Even if the person is not addicted, given the omnipresence of cyber space, too much time online can start to affect sleeping patterns, and thus have an impact on the person's ability to function during the day-time.

At this moment there are ever-increasing numbers of adolescents with ASD who are 'school refusals' due to anxiety, bullying and sensory issues. Many of this cohort revert to the online world while at home. With hours to while away each day, many will drift into staying online into the night then finding it very difficult to have a structure or focus to their days. We recommend that it is imperative that people with ASD keep a structure and routine to their days and nights. If out of school, on a break from college or unemployed, people with ASD should find a focus to their days that involves interactions with others (ideally this should include interactions outside of the immediate family). This is vital as it creates a balance between online and 'real world' interactions. It is very often the case that the less people with ASD interact with others face to face, the more difficult these interactions become. This principle also extends to the spaces people meet in and the sensory implications of these spaces. It is also true that absolute avoidance of sensorily problematic social or public spaces (especially school, college, work spaces) may be appealing in the short term but ultimately lead to larger issues in the long term. For instance, being out of school, college or work will in most cases have a detrimental effect on people's self-esteem and confidence.

Another potential advantage of cyber space is its use as a method of finding employment or being employed. Cyber space may work as a space in which people can conduct their work without having to contend with the potential anxieties and sensory difficulties associated with many conventional workplaces. The virtual workplace is one which may or may not have colleagues to interact with, deadlines to be met, bosses to please; however, all of these transactions can be potentially carried out in front of a computer in the home. We again advise that this should not be to the detriment of face-to-face interactions with people socially; it may be a way for people who are unable to tolerate the conventional workplace to have employment. If this is the case then it is very important that the person with ASD find social outlets in their lives generally to counteract the lack of social interaction that may be occurring in the workplace. This may mean meeting friends and joining clubs, for instance.

Creating and developing sensory capital

Throughout the course of this book, we have discussed the principle of broadening or increasing the space that people with autism can manage and this is another example of the importance of the person not allowing their world to become shrunken because of sensory issues. If the person is more comfortable working online then it is often useful to look at this as creating sensory capital.[2] In other words, the sensory anxieties that may have occurred in the workplace are avoided and therefore the person with ASD has saved up their sensory capital to be used in a different environment, i.e. a social environment. If the person does not recognise, maintain or develop their sensory capital then it will dwindle away and invariably they will find that every space they interact with creates sensory difficulties. To build this point further, as a general principle sensory capital can be built up even if the person is in a 'conventional' workplace. This is achieved through hard work, determination and stamina – the more the person gets used to different sensory environments, the more they should develop the strategies needed to manage these environments and thus the more sensory capital built which can also be drawn on to manage other sensory environments.

---

2   We will define sensory capital as a well of sensory experiences, sensory strategies, energy and will.

CONCLUSION

Autism is evolving constantly in terms of how it is understood by the general public, parents, the media and researchers/the medical community. There has been a significant increase in the numbers of research papers, books, movies and media articles on the subject. Much of this is driven by the increasing amount of people with autism representing themselves through public fora. More pertinently people with autism have been increasingly representing themselves online and have begun to create a recognisable autism community (or maybe better described as communities). This evolution of the autism community online allows for people with autism across the world to share experiences, discuss ideas, make friends (and sometimes enemies) all through a medium that circumvents anxieties and sensory issues that may be present in most face-to-face or conventional interactions. We have previously discussed the potential pros and cons of using cyber space as a method by which to interact with others but it is undeniable that cyber space has been integral to the creation of an online community and this is to be welcomed. It has also had a knock-on effect on other media sources with ever more TV shows in particular featuring characters with autism.

What is vital however is that people on the AS do not get excluded from 'real' spaces and instead feel that they only belong in cyber space with cyber space being seen as 'their' space. While it can be an incredibly positive and impactful media by which people with autism can coalesce and represent themselves, this should not mean that other spaces gradually become off limits. If this were to be the case, many would argue, regular spaces – public, social and private – may begin to become less flexible towards sensory or 'behavioural' difference; in fact these spaces could become ever more imbued with the culture of 'normality', a culture that rejects behaviours or needs deemed aberrant. The creation of a sensory environment that is based on a shared pluralist[1] culture is vital for people with ASD. The more that people with ASD feel they are 'aberrant' or unwelcome in these spaces, the more likely they will withdraw to other spaces and the less chance of any useful change occurring in mainstream spaces.

The creation of a pluralist sensory culture must begin with education and in educational settings. The recognition of sensory issues as being a primary feature of autism in the DSM-5 is to be welcomed but education needs to go further than the medical field. Education should begin with awareness training for all public services and services that deal with people who may have sensory issues, including all educational settings, hospitals, etc. The creation of a universal design for schools should include its sensory architecture. Rather than just including the physical structure of the school its sensory architecture should include a recognition of the sensory strategies that should be created and tailored to meet the individual needs of students.

The sensory advantage

A significant feature in the neurotypical social construction of the autistic person is the idea of difference. We have previously

---

1   Pluralist in creating a sensory culture that recognises difference from 'normal' sensory profiles.

discussed at length the notion of culturally created 'norms' and the ways in which people with autism may not fit into these categories. What is interesting is the duality of ways in which sensory differences are perceived by people with autism as well as neurotypicals. On the one hand, sensory differences are fundamental to the autism self-identity. On the other hand, there are numerous ways in which sensory differences play into the perception of difference by neurotypicals of people with autism (including meltdowns and hearing sounds more loudly). What this means is that many people with autism may not necessarily look at sensory differences as being a discrete part of their identity; rather that sensory differences are a component part of varying significance in the autistic person's experience of the world. If, as philosophical empiricism suggests, knowledge and our understanding of reality comes from sensory experience then it stands to reason that people with autism often have a uniquely individual perception of the world which may be both difficult and exhilarating and this is what we may term the sensory advantage.

Interviewee A discusses the positive aspects of his sensory differences by describing the pleasure derived from observing the patterns created by swirling water in a river or stream. This is in fact as pleasurable to him as others may find a book or music in that he becomes immersed in his observation to the point of shutting other perceptions out. In these moments his ability to distinguish pleasurable patterns in a way that most neurotypicals would not be capable of, or enjoy, is indicative of the benefits of sensory difference. It also ties in with Mottron *et al.*'s 2006 study on how people with autism may have greater perceptual ability in the areas of pattern detection, visual memories and musical talent.

This also ties in with Interviewee B who is a singer and musician. His ability to see patterns allied to his perfect pitch has assisted him in being able to innately understand the structure of music and therefore play musical instruments with relative ease. Combined with this is his ability to perform Parkour (essentially using the city/street scape to perform acts of agility and skill, it is based on the idea of always maintaining movement and momentum and often involves using physical structures as devices by which to propel oneself). He feels that his desire to perform Parkour was fundamentally informed by his need for sensory stimulation. The architecture of the street provides perfect spaces in which his sensory needs can be played out; it also helps that it is an exhilarating activity that promotes physical health. Essential to the philosophy of Parkour is perceiving street architecture in ways that move beyond their initial purpose. This also means having the ability to use the physical features of the urban landscape in ways that they were not originally designed for. In this perspective, for example, a wall is no longer a barrier that prevents movement from one space to another; rather it is a platform which can be used to gain the momentum needed to traverse different spaces. This example is carefully chosen to be representative of the idea of autism as being a fortress, where there is a real person trying to escape the impenetrable walls that surround them, such as Bruno Bettelheim's *The Empty Fortress* (1967).

A further aspect of Parkour that is appealing to the interviewee is that it allows him to articulate his sensory needs in a more 'acceptable' manner. It provides a physical platform by which he can not only express his sensory needs but also his physical and creative needs. A final thought on how this activity has benefited the interviewee is that it provides a 'counter-cultural' community which he feels part of. In this community he is not questioned as to why he may require the sensory inputs gained from Parkour; rather he is admired for his skill, strength, agility and bravery. This also provides a social space which is based on a common activity and which has less focus on social interaction. It is the perfect vehicle by which to express his sensory needs, and articulate his sensory differences in a community that welcomes and applauds his 'differences'.

What the examples before show is the ways in which sensory differences can be pleasurable or can be harnessed to become pleasurable. They also show how sensory differences, which may be deemed as outside the 'norm' by many neurotypicals, can be part of perceiving the world in unique ways and should be addressed, welcomed or encouraged depending on the needs of each person with autism. Throughout the book we have made some reference to philosophy. This is because philosophy speaks to us about the nature of reality and what it means to be human. This is especially pertinent in terms of people with autism and sensory differences. For example, if it is true that there is no defined reality, only our perceptions of same, what does this mean for people with sensory differences? We could surmise that people with sensory differences live in an unreality, are disconnected from the real world and that their perceptions should be adjusted to suit the ways in which the world is organised by people without sensory differences. However, we would argue that the sensory differences associated with autism provide a version of reality that may in fact be more real than people without sensory differences – for example, people who have enhanced perceptual functioning which may allow for earlier and easier acquisition of reading skills, ability to spot patterns that others may not find (though this is also attributed to weak central coherence – focusing on the minutiae rather than the whole), or enhanced visual memory as in the case of Temple Grandin, Stephen Wiltshire and Jesse Park (Solomon 2010).

These abilities often allow the person to perceive the world in ways that most people without sensory differences cannot, for example Temple Grandin's ability to recall memories in picture form. It could be argued that this is a more real reality, as opposed to a deficit in functioning that distorts reality.

Summary of strategies

There are three overarching strands to this book: the strategies that people with autism can apply to their daily lives to mediate against the sensory difficulties they may experience in different environments; that sensory differences can often be mediated for and addressed through the creation of more suitable sensory architecture; and that a greater understanding of the sensory and other needs of people with autism can help in the creation of a more diverse culture that accepts difference in all its manifestations. To borrow a related idea: 'The best way of responding to the harm done by high levels of inequality would be to reduce inequality itself...reducing inequality would increase the wellbeing and quality of life for all of us' (Wilkinson and Pickett 2009, p.33).

In terms of the specific strategies that we have suggested in this book, we have endeavoured to make them as practical, adaptable, broad ranging and prescient as possible. This also means that there are general suggestions which can be broken down and individualised for each person's own needs. The overall Sensory Strategy is created to try and meet the sensory needs that people with ASD will encounter across their lives through different environments, from school to college and work, and from home to public and social spaces also incorporating travel. This is not meant to be an exhaustive list; rather it is an attempt to cover as many different environments as possible in a generalised way. The Sensory Strategy is broken into component parts designed to address specific environments. For example, the Learning Plan incorporates the sensory needs of students while also addressing social communication and interactive needs. The plan for the workplace similarly aims to address not only the sensory needs but also some of the other needs that people with autism may have in the workplace, such as whether to disclose their autism and the potential benefits or negatives attached to that decision. The Sensory Strategy addresses the home lives of people with ASD, their partners and children. In this section we aim to provide practical strategies for people in terms of their sensory needs and how this may apply to relationships, sharing homes and having children. Its intention is to provide suggestions to people from the perspective of the person with autism, their neurotypical partner or spouse, couples with autism and children with autism.

ASD sensory issues and the future

Given the relatively recent recognition of the part sensory issues play in the experience of autism, I would hope that we are now on the precipice of a new understanding of autism. Allied to this there are increased opportunities for people with autism to represent themselves in the public arena and perhaps it is this rather than any other means that is going to affect how people with autism are understood by neurotypical society. This is not to diminish the importance of social policy in terms of how people with autism experience the world and are treated by the state. The enactment of legislature which begins to address the complex needs of a heterogeneous community is vital to the future of people living with autism and those yet to be born. In terms of social policy, it is imperative that awareness training should feature as a requirement and that this awareness training should incorporate how a person's sensory differences may manifest, and the ways in which these differences may be addressed. Awareness of sensory needs should begin at school.

Many generations of people with autism have talked and written about the negative experience of school and its repercussions. We have aimed to try and address this issue in Chapter 3 in terms of the sense–memory–emotion paradigm. People with autism are just as emotional and just as likely to feel pain, hurt, joy, love and fear as neurotypicals are; they may not express it in the same ways but this should not be assumed as meaning a lack of emotion. The experience of school for many people with autism is a fundamental one which resonates throughout their lives, particularly if it is a negative experience. These negative experiences can have echoes that may affect people with ASD in workplaces and other environments across their life course. We cannot, therefore, simply talk of sensory issues, anxiety, social communication issues or residual/historical emotional issues in isolation from each other as to do so would be to suggest that a person with autism is not the sum of their parts, that rather they are a multitude of diagnostic criteria, a mass of deficits. School, then, is instrumental in how people with autism will experience their first major public space. This means that having awareness of autism, creating inclusive sensory architecture, providing for sensory diversity and creating individualised Learning Plans is a responsibility that schools have to children with sensory differences.

The workplace has evolved into an adaptable space that is no longer necessarily rooted to a physical structure. Work can and increasingly does take place anywhere and at any time. With each passing year the divisions between our public and private selves, as well as our work and private lives, have become ever more fluid to the point that we are rarely completely removed from work due to the accessibility of cyber space through so many different media now, and we are rarely completely away from some sort of interaction for the same reasons. The possibility of working from home, or any other space that is not shared with colleagues, offers exciting opportunities for people with ASD and sensory issues. This diversity is very welcome in the ways in which it represents these opportunities for employment that would not have been possible in the past; however, it could be argued that it may also be (unknowingly) representative of a sense in the neurotypical community that cyber space is a 'more suitable' space for people with autism. This is undoubtedly a complex issue as the positives of cyber space for people with autism are undeniable, yet it cannot be the case that cyber space becomes a reductive space that in some ways diminishes the possibilities for face-to-face contact for people with ASD, or that allows society and the state to abdicate its responsibility in terms of encouraging diversity in all its forms. This should also extend to employers. While we have established that it is not the sole responsibility of employers to recognise diversity, employers should be prepared to accept ways in which the workplace can be made more sensorily diverse, or ways in which the sensory needs of employees can be met through flexibility and a willingness to support the employee.

Ultimately, the future for people with ASD looks increasingly more positive. The greater awareness we have just discussed allied to more recognition of the needs of people with autism by the state has meant that the dark days of people with autism being misdiagnosed or mistreated are beginning to become a thing of the past. This is not to say that all the rights of people with autism have been met. There is still some way to go for that to be the case and looking globally at the issues facing people with autism from lack of understanding, to religious, cultural or socio-economics, we can clearly see that the quest for rights will continue. The recognition of sensory difference, however, is a further example of the ways in which the needs of people with autism are beginning to be understood. We have touched on the positive philosophical perspective of sensory differences for people with autism as well as the practical everyday positives that are derived from sensory difference. It is this aspect of sensory difference that may be cause for most optimism; while we cannot deny the real difficulties attached to some sensory differences, the positives of sensory difference for people with autism have the potential to provide different perspectives and insights on the world, to perceive the world differently in ways that may be enlightening and uplifting for society at large.

REFERENCES

American Psychiatric Association (2013) *Diagnostic and Statistical Manual of Mental Disorders*, 5th edition. Washington, DC: APA.

Andari, E, Duhamel, J. R., Zalla, T., Herbrecht, E., Leboyer, M. and Sirigu, A. (2010) 'Promoting social behavior with oxytocin in high-functioning autism spectrum disorders.' *Proceedings of the National Academy of Sciences US 107*, 4389–4394.

AOTA (2011) *Children and Adolescents with Challenges in Sensory Processing and Sensory Integration.* Bethesda, MD: American Occupational Therapy Association.

Armstrong, T. (2010) *Neurodiversity: Discovering the Extraordinary Gifts of Autism, ADHD, Dyslexia, and Other Brain Differences.* Cambridge: Da Capo Press.

Asher, J. E., Lamb, J. A., Brocklebank, D., Cazier, J.-B., Maestrini, E., Addis, L. et al. (2009) 'A whole-genome scan and fine-mapping linkage study of auditory-visual synesthesia reveals evidence of linkage to chromosomes 2q24, 5q33, 6p12, and 12p12'. *American Journal of Human Genetics 84*, 279–285.

Ayres, A. J. (1972) *Sensory Integration and Learning Disorders.* Los Angeles, CA: Western Psychological Services.

Ayres, A. J. (2004) *Sensory Integration and Praxis Tests Manual: Updated Edition.* Los Angeles, CA: Western Psychological Services.

Baranek, G. T., David, F. J., Poe, M. D., Stone, W. L., Watson, L. R. (2006) 'Sensory Experiences Questionnaire: Discriminating sensory features in young children with autism, developmental delays, and typical development.' *Journal of Child Psychology and Psychiatry 47*, 6, 591–601.

Baranek, G. T. (2002) 'Efficacy of sensory and motor interventions for children with autism.' *Journal of Autism and Developmental Disorders 32*, 5, 397–422.

Baron-Cohen, S. (2000) *Is Asperger Syndrome Necessarily a Disability?* Available at http://docs.autismresearchcentre.com/papers/2002_BC_ASDisability.pdf, accessed on 27 November 2015.

Baron Cohen, S., Bor, D., Billington, J., Asher, J., Wheelwright, S. and Ashwin, C. (2007) 'Savant memory in a man with colour-number synaesthesia and Asperger Syndrome.' *Journal of Consciousness Studies 14*, 237–251.

Baron-Cohen, S., Johnson, D., Asher, J., Wheelwright, S., Fisher, S., Gregersen, P. and Allison, C. (2013) 'Is synaesthesia more common in autism?' *Molecular Autism 4*, 40.

Bauminger, N. and Kasari, C. (2000) 'Loneliness and friendship in high-functioning children with autism.' *Child Development 71*, 447–456.

Benetto, L., Kuschner, E. S. and Hyman, S. L. (2007) 'Olfaction and taste processing in autism.' *Biological Psychiatry 62*, 1015–1021.

Ben-Sasson, A., Len, L., Fluss, R., Cermak, S. A., Engel-Yeger, B. and Gal, E. (2009) 'A meta-analysis of sensory modulation symptoms in individuals with autism spectrum disorders.' *Journal of Autism and Development Disorders 39*, 1, 1–11.

Bernstein, D. and Rubin, D. C. (2002) 'Emotionally charged autobiographical memories across the lifespan: The retention of happy, sad, traumatic, and involuntary memories.' *Psychology and Aging 17*, 636–652.

Bettelheim, B. (1967) *The Empty Fortress: Infantile Autism and the Birth of Self.* New York: Free Press.

Bogdashina, O. (2003) *Sensory Perceptual Issues in Autism and Asperger Syndrome.* London: Jessica Kingsley Publishers.

Bond, L. Carlin, J. Thomas, J. Rubin, K. Patton, G. (2001) 'Does bullying cause emotional problems? A prospective study of young teenagers' *British Medical Journal, 1*, 323, 7311, 480–484.

Brown-Lavoie, S. M., Viecili, M. A. and Weiss, J. A. (2014) 'Sexual knowledge and victimization in adults with autism spectrum disorders'. *Journal of Autism and Developmental Disorders 44*, 9, 2185–2196.

Buchanan, T. W. (2007) 'Retrieval of emotional memories.' *American Psychological Association 133*, 5, 761–779.

Carley, M. J. (2008) *Asperger's from the Inside Out.* New York: Penguin.

Cemak, S. A., Curtin, C. and Bandini, L. G. (2010) 'Food selectivity and sensory sensitivity in children with autism spectrum disorders.' *Journal of the American Dietetic Association 110*, 238–246.

Chou, C., Condron, L. and Belland, J. C. (2005) 'A review of the research on Internet addiction.' *Educational Psychology Review 17*, 4, 363–388.

Coch, D., Fischer, K. W. and Dawson, G. (eds) (2007) *Human Behavior, Learning, and the Developing Brain: Typical Development.* New York: Guilford Press.

Collins, P. (2004) *Not Even Wrong: A Father's Journey into the Lost History of Autism.* New York and London: Bloomsbury.

Courchesne, E. and Pierce K. (2005a) 'Why the frontal cortex in autism might be talking only to itself: Local over-connectivity but long-distance disconnection.' *Current Opinion in Neurobiology 15*, 2, 225–230.

Courchesne E. and Pierce K. (2005b) 'Brain overgrowth in autism during a critical time in development: Implications for frontal pyramidal neuron and interneuron development and connectivity.' *International Journal of Developmental Neuroscience 23*, 2–3, 153–170.

Crane, L. and Goddard, L. (2008) 'Episodic and semantic autobiographical memory in adults with Autism Spectrum Disorders.' *Journal of Autism and Developmental Disorders 38*, 3, 498–506.

Crane, L., Goddard, L. and Pring, L. (2009) 'Sensory processing in adults with autism spectrum disorders.' *Autism 13*, 3, 215–228.

Crooks, V. (2010) 'Women's Changing Experiences of the Home and Life Inside it After Becoming Chronically Ill.' In V. Chouinard, E. Hall and R. Wilton (eds) *Towards Enabling Geographies: 'Disabled' Bodies and Minds in Society and Space*. Surrey: Ashgate Publishing Limited.

Davidson, J. and Henderson, V. (2010) 'Travel in parallel with us for a while: Sensory geographies of autism.' *The Canadian Geographer 54*, 4, 462–475.

Davidson, J. and Parr, H. (2010) 'Enabling cultures of dis/order online', in V. Chouinard, E. Hall and R. Wilton (eds) *Towards Enabling Geographies: 'Disabled' Bodies and Minds in Society and Space*. Surrey: Ashgate Publishing Limited.

DePape, A. M., Hall, G. and Tillman, B. (2012) 'Auditory processing in high functioning adolescents with autism spectrum disorder.' *Plos One 7*, 9.

Dubin, N. (2009) *Asperger Syndrome and Anxiety: A Successful Guide to Successful Stress Management*. London: Jessica Kingsley Publishers.

Dunn, W. (1999) *The Sensory Profile*. San Antonio, TX: PsychCorp.

Dunn, W. (2007) 'Ecology of Human Performance Model.' In S. Dunbar (ed.) *Occupational Therapy Models for Intervention with Children and Families*. Thorofare, NJ: Slack Inc., pp.127–156.

Dunn, W., Myles, B. and Orr, S. (2002) 'Sensory processing issues associated with Asperger syndrome: A preliminary investigation.' *American Journal of Occupational Therapy 56*, 97–102.

Editors of Time-Life (1994) *Emotions*. Alexandria, VA: Time-Life Books.

Fantz, R. L. (1961) 'The origin of form perception.' *Scientific American 204*, 5, 66–72.

Ferguson, C. J., Coulson, M. and Barnett, J. (2011) 'A meta analysis of pathological gaming prevalence and co-morbidity with mental health, academic and social problems.' *Journal of Psychiatric Research 45*, 12, 1573–1578.

Frith, U. (1989) *Autism: Explaining the Enigma*. Oxford: Basil Blackwell.

Gazzaniga, M.S. and Heatherton, T. (2006) *Psychological Science: Mind, Brain, and Behavior, 2nd edition*. New York: W. W. Norton.

Gerland, G. (2003) *A Real Person: Life on the Outside.* London: Souvenir Press.

Goffman, E. (1963a) *Behaviour in Public Places.* New York: The Free Press of Glencoe.

Goffman, E. (1963b) *Stigma: Notes on the Management of Spoiled Identity.* London: Penguin.

Grandin, T. (2006) *Thinking in Pictures: My Life with Autism.* New York: Vintage.

Grandin, T. and Scariano, M. (1986) *Emergence: Labeled Autistic.* Navato, CA: Arena Press.

Griffiths, M. D. and Hunt, N. (1998) 'Dependence on computer games by adolescence.' *Psychological Reports 82*, 2, 475–480.

Hall, E. (2004) 'Social geography of learning difficulties: Narratives of exclusion and inclusion.' *Area 36*, 3, 298–306.

Hall, S. (1991) 'Old and New Identities, Old and New Ethnicities.' In A. King (ed.) *Culture, Globalization and the World System.* New York: State University of New York, Department of Art and Art History.

Haq, I. and Le Couteur, A. (2004) 'Autism Spectrum Disorder.' *Medicine 32*, 61–63.

Henault, I. (2006) *Asperger Syndrome and Sexuality: From Adolescence through Adulthood.* London: Jessica Kingsley Publishers.

Higashida, N. (2013) *The Reason I Jump: One Boy's Voice from the Silence of Autism.* London: Hodder and Stoughton Ltd.

Hock, R. R. (2013) *Forty Studies that Changed Psychology: Explorations into the History of Psychological Research.* Upper Saddle River, NJ: Pearson/Prentice Hall.

Hofmann, S. G. and Bitran, S. (2007) 'Sensory-processing sensitivity in social anxiety disorder: Relationship to harm avoidance and diagnostic subtypes.' *Journal of Anxiety Disorders 21*, 944–954.

Holliday Willey, J. (1999) *Pretending to be Normal: Living with Asperger's Syndrome.* London: Jessica Kingsley Publishers.

Johnston, R. J. (1979) *Geography and Geographers: Anglo American Human Geography Since 1945.* London: Arnold.

Kandel, E. R., Schwartz, J. H. and Jessell, T. M. (2000) *Principles of Neural Science, 4th edition.* New York: McGraw-Hill.

Kemner, C., Verbaten, M. N., Cuperus, J. M., Camfferman, G. and van Engeland, H. (1995) 'Auditory event-related brain potentials in autistic children and three different control groups'. *Biological Psychiatry 38*, 150–165.

Kerkhof, P., Finkenauer, C. and Muusses, L. D. (2011) 'Relational consequences of compulsive Internet use: A longitudinal study among newlyweds.' *Human Communication Research 37*, 2, 147–173.

Kitchin, R. (1998) 'Out of place, knowing one's place: Space, power and exclusion of disabled people.' *Disability and Society 13*, 3, 343–356.

Klin, A., Volkmar, F. R. and Sparrow, S. (2000) *Asperger Syndrome*. London: The Guilford Press.

Kuhanek, H. M. and Watling, R. (2010) *Autism: A Comprehensive Occupational Therapy Approach*. Bethesda, MD: American Occupational Therapy Association, Inc.

Lane, A. E., Dennis, S. J. and Geraghty, M. E. (2011) 'Brief report: Further evidence of sensory subtypes in autism.' *Journal of Autism and Development Disorders 41*, 826–831.

Marks, L. E. (1978) *The Unity of the Senses: Interrelations among the Modalities*. New York, NY: Academic Press.

Mayes, S., Calhoun, S., Mayes, D. and Molitoris, S. (1999) 'Autism and ADHD: Overlapping and discriminating symptoms.' *Research in Autism Spectrum Disorders 6*, 1, 277–285.

Mayes, S. Calhoun, S., Mayes, D. and Molitaris, S. (2012) 'Autism and ADHD: Overlapping and discriminating symptoms.' *Research in Autism Spectrum Disorders, 6*, 1, 277–285.

Mazurek, M. and Wenstrup, C. (2013) 'Television, video game and social media use among children with ASD and typically developing siblings.' *Journal of Autism and Development Disorders 43*, 1258–1271.

Mazurek, M., Shattuck, P., Wagner, M. and Cooper, B. (2012) 'Prevalence and correlates of screen based media use among youths with autism spectrum disorders.' *Journal of Autism and Developmental Disorders 42*, 1757–1767.

Meerkerk, G. J., Van Den Eijnden, R., Vermulst, A. A. et al. (2009) 'The compulsive Internet use scale (CIUS): Some psychometric properties.' *Cyberpsychology and Behavior 12*, 1, 1–6.

Melzack, R. and Wall, P. (1982) *The Challenge of Pain*. Harmondsworth: Penguin.

Mildner, V. (2008) *The Cognitive Neuroscience of Human Communication*. New York: Lawrence Erlbaum Associates.

Miller, L. J., Anzalone, M. E., Lane, S. J., Cermak, S. A. and Osten, E. T. (2007) 'Concept evolution in sensory integration: A proposed nosology for diagnosis.' *American Journal of Occupational Therapy 61*, 2, 135–40.

Moloney, P. (2010) 'How can a chord be weird if it expresses your soul? Some critical reflections on the diagnosis of Asperger's syndrome.' *Disability and Society 25*, 2, 135–148.

Morahan-Martin, J. and Schumacher, P. (2000) 'Incidence and correlates of pathological Internet use among college students.' *Computers in Human Behavior 16*, 1, 13–29.

Nadon, G., Feldman, D. E., Dunn, W. and Gisel, E. (2011) 'Association of sensory processing and eating problems in children with autism spectrum disorders.' *Autism Research and Treatment 541926*.

Occelli V., Esposito, G., Venuti, P., Arduino, G. M. and Zampini, M. (2013) 'The Takete-Maluma phenomenon in autism spectrum disorders.' *Perception 42*, 2, 233–41.

Parsons, S. and Mitchell, P. (2002) 'The potential of virtual reality in social skills training for people with autistic spectrum disorders.' *Journal of Intellectual Disability Research 46*, 5, 430–443.

Paton, B., Hohwy, J. and Enticott, P. G. (2012) 'The rubber hand illusion reveals proprioceptive and sensorimotor differences in autism spectrum disorders.' *Journal of Autism and Development Disorders 42*, 9, 1870–83.

Prince-Hughes, D. (2004) *Songs of the Gorilla Nation: My Journey Through Autism*. New York: Three Rivers.

Purves, D., Augustine, G., Fitzpatrick, D., Hall, W., LaMantia, A. S. and White, L. E. (2012) *Principles of Cognitive Neuroscience, 5th edition*. Sunderland, MA: Sinauer Associates.

Purves, D., Augustine, G. J., Fitzpatrick, D., Hall, W. C., La Mantia, A. S., McNamara, J. O. and White, L. E. (2008) *Neuroscience*. Sunderland, MA: Sinauer Associates.

Purves, D., Brannon, M., Cabeza, R., Huettal, S., LaBar, K., Platt, M. and Woldorff, M. (2008) *Principles of Cognitive Neuroscience*. Sunderland, MA: Sinauer Associates.

Reber, A. S. (1985) *Dictionary of Psychology*. London: Penguin.

Reisman, J. and Hanschu, B. (1992) *Sensory Integration Inventory-Revised for Individuals with Developmental Disabilities*. Hugo, MN: PDP Inc. Press.

Roekel, E. Van, Scholte, R. H. and Didden, R. (2010) 'Bullying among adolescents with autism spectrum disorders: prevalence and perception.' *Journal of Autism and Developmental Disorders 40*, 63–73.

Rogers, S. J. and Ozonoff, S. (2005) 'What do we know about sensory dysfunction in autism? A critical review of the empirical evidence.' *Journal of Child Psychology and Psychiatry 46*, 12, 1255–68.

Ross, P. (2008) 'Common sense about qualities and senses.' *Philosophical Studies 138*, 3, 299–316.

Roth, M. and Gillis, J. (2014) 'Convenience with the click of a mouse: A survey of adults with Autism Spectrum Disorder on online dating.' *Sexuality and Disability 33*, 1, 133–150.

Sanders, C. E., Field, T. M., Diego, M. et al. (2000) 'The relationship of Internet use to depression and social isolation among adolescents.' *Adolescence 35*, 138, 237–242.

Schneider, G. E. (1969) 'Two visual systems.' *Science 163*, 3870, 895–902.

Schoen, S. A., Miler, L. J., Brett-Green, B. A. and Nielsen, D. M. (2009) 'Physiological and behavioural differences in sensory processing: A comparison of children with autism spectrum disorder and sensory modulation disorder.' *Frontiers in Integrative Neuroscience 3*, 29.

Sharif, I. and Sargent, J. D. (2006) 'Association between television, movie, and video game exposure and school performance.' *Pediatrics 118*, 4, 1061–1070.

Sharif, I., Wills, T. A. and Sargent, J. D. (2010) 'Effect of visual media use on school performance: A prospective study.' *Journal of Adolescent Health 46*, 1, 52–61.

Shoener, R., Kinnealey, M. and Koenig, K. (2008) 'You can know me now if you listen: Sensory, motor, and communication issues in a nonverbal person with autism.' *American Journal of Occupational Therapy 62*, 547–553.

Shore, S. (2003) *Beyond the Wall: Personal Experiences with Autism and Asperger Syndrome*. Kansas: Autism Asperger Publishing Limited.

Siegel, A., Sapru, H. and Siegel, H. (2006) *Essential Neuroscience*. Philadelphia: Lippincott Williams & Wilkins.

Simone, R. (2010) *Aspergirls: Empowering Females with Asperger Syndrome*. London: Jessica Kingsley Publishers.

Solomon, O. (2010) 'Sense and the senses: Anthropology and the study of autism.' *Annual Review of Anthropology 39*, 241–259.

Suzuki, Y., Critchley, H. C., Rowe, A., Howlin, P. and Murphy, D. G. M. (2003) 'Impaired olfactory identification in Asperger's syndrome' *Journal of Neuropsychiatry and Clinical Neuroscience 15*, 105–107.

Tammet, D. (2006) *Born on a Blue Day*. London: Hodder & Stoughton.

Tammet, D. (2009) *Embracing the Wide Sky*. London: Hodder & Stoughton.

Tantam, D. (2009) *Can the World Afford Autistic Spectrum Disorder? Nonverbal Communication, Asperger Syndrome and the Interbrain*. London: Jessica Kingsley Publishers.

Tanweer, T., Rathbone, C. and Souchay, C. (2010) 'Autobiographical memory, autonoetic consciousness, and identity in Asperger Syndrome.' *Neuropsychologia 48*, 4, 900–908.

Tavassoli, T., Auyeung, B., Murphy, L., Baron-Cohen, S. and Chakrabarti, B. (2012) 'Variation in the autism candidate gene GABRB3 modulates tactile sensitivity in typically developing children.' *Molecular Autism 3*, 6.

Terkenli, T. (1995) 'Home as a region.' *Geographical Review 85*, 3, 324–334.

Tomchek, S. and Case-Smith, J. (2009) *Occupational Therapy Practice Guidelines for Children and Adults with Autism*. Bethesda, MD: AOTA Press.

Tuan, Y. F. (1991) 'A view of geography.' *Geographical Review 81*, 1, 99–107.

Van Den Eijnden, R. J., Meerkerk, G.J., Vermulst, A. A. et al. (2008) 'Online communication, compulsive Internet use, and psychosocial well being among adolescents: A longitudinal study.' *Developmental Psychology 44*, 3, 655.

Ward, J. and Simner, J. (2005) 'Is synaesthesia an X-linked dominant trait with lethality in males?' *Perception 34*, 5, 611–623.

Ward J., Huckstep, B. and Tsakanikos, E. (2006) 'Sound-colour synaesthesia: To what extent does it use cross-modal mechanisms common to us all?' *Cognition 42*, 264–280.

Williams, D. (1992) *Nobody Nowhere*. London: Jessica Kingsley Publishers.

Williams, D. (1999) *Nobody Nowhere*. London: Jessica Kingsley Publishers.

Wilkinson, R. and Pickett, K. (2009) *The Spirit Level: Why Equality is Better for Everyone*. London: Penguin.

Winnicott, D. (1960) 'The theory of the parent-child relationship.' *International Journal of Psychoanalysis 41*, 585–595.

Wolf, N. (2012) *Vagina: A New Biography*. London: Virago.

FURTHER READING

Asperger, H. (1938) 'The mentally abnormal child.' *Viennese Clinical Weekly* 49, 1–12.

Asperger, H. (1944) 'Die autistischen Psychopathen im Kindesalter.' *Archiv fur Psychiatrie und Nervenkrankheiten No 177*, 76–137. In M. Ghaziuddin (2005) *Mental Health Aspects of Autism and Asperger Syndrome.* London: Jessica Kingsley Publishers.

Atkinson, D., Jackson, M. and Walmsley, J. (1997) *Forgotten Lives: Exploring the History of Learning Disability.* Kidderminster: Bild Publications.

Attwood, T. (2007) *The Complete Guide to Asperger's Syndrome.* London: Jessica Kingsley Publishers.

Balfe, M., Chen, T. and Tantam, D. (2005) *Sheffield Survey of Health and Social Care Needs of Adolescents and Adults with Asperger Syndrome.* Sheffield: School of Health and Related Research.

Baron-Cohen, S. (1995) *Mind Blindness: An Essay on Autism and Theory of Mind.* Cambridge, MA: MIT Press.

Baron-Cohen, S. (2008) *Autism and Asperger Syndrome.* Oxford: Oxford University Press.

Batten, A., Corbett, C., Rosenblatt, M., Withers, L. and Yuille, R. (2006) *Make School Make Sense: Autism and Education, the Reality for Families Today.* London: National Autistic Society.

Baudrillard, J. (1989) *The Consumer Society: Myths and Structures.* London: Sage.

Baudrillard, J. (1989) *The Consumer Society: Myths and Structures.* London: Sage

Beardon, L. and Edmonds, G. (2007) *Aspect Consultancy Report: A National Report on the Needs of Adults with Asperger Syndrome.* Available at http:// researchautism.net/publications/3359/aspect-consultancy-report.-a-national-report-on-the-needs-of-adults-with-asperger-syndrome. Accessed on 30 December 2015.

Billington, T. (2006) 'Working with autistic children and young people: Sense, experience and the challenges for services, policies and practices.' *Disability and Society 21*, 1, 1–13.

Birnie, J. (2006) 'Developing an Inclusive Curriculum for Students with Asperger Syndrome.' In J. Leach and J. Birnie (eds) *Developing an Inclusive Curriculum for (a) Students with Mental Health Issues (b) Students with Asperger Syndrome*. Cheltenham: Geography Discipline Network, pp.85–107.

Blunt, A. and Varley, A. (2004) 'Geographies of home: An introduction.' *Cultural Geographies 11*, 3–6.

Bogdashina, O. (2006) *Theory of Mind and the Triad of Perspectives on Autism and Asperger Syndrome: A View from the Bridge*. London: Jessica Kingsley Publishers.

Bogdashina, O. (2010) *Autism and the Edges of the Known World: Sensitivities, Language and Constructed Reality*. London: Jessica Kingsley Publishers.

Bumiler, K. (2008) 'Quirky citizens: Autism, gender, and reimagining disability.' *Signs 33*, 4, 967–991.

Burns, T. (1992) *Erving Goffman*. London: Routledge.

Butler, R. and Bowlby, S. (1995) 'Disabled bodies in public space.' *Geographical Paper Series B*. Reading: University of Reading.

Butler, R. and Bowlby, S. (1997) 'Bodies and spaces: An exploration of disabled people's experiences of public spaces.' *Environment and Planning D: Society and Space 15*, 411–434.

Butler, R. and Parr, H. (eds) (1999) *Mind and Body Spaces: Geographies of Illness, Impairment and Disability*. London: Routledge.

Carter, E., Donald, J. and Squires, J. (1993) *Space and Place: Theories of Identity and Location*. London: Lawrence & Wishart Limited.

Cemak, S. A., Curtin, C. and Bandini, L. G. (2010) 'Food selectivity and sensory sensitivity in children with autism spectrum disorders.' *Journal of the American Dietetic Association 110*, 238–246.

Chouinard, V. (1997) 'Making space for disabling difference: challenging ableist geographies.' *Environment and Planning D: Society and Space 15*, 379–387.

Chouinard, V., Hall, E. and Wilton, R. (2010) *Towards Enabling Geographies: Disabled Bodies and Minds in Society and Space*. Surrey: Ashgate Publishing Ltd.

Cleary, S. D. (2000) 'Adolescent victimization and associated suicidal and violent behaviours.' *Adolescence 35*, 671–682.

Conlon, D. (2004) 'Productive bodies, performative spaces: everyday life in Christopher Park.' *Sexualities 7*, 462–479.

Conrad, P. (1992) 'Medicalization and social control.' *Annual Review of Sociology 18*, 209–232.

Conrad, P. (2005) 'The shifting engines of medicalization.' *Journal of Health and Social Behaviour 46*, 3–14.

Cox, K. R. and Golledge, R. G. (1981) *Behavioural Problems in Geography Revisited*. London: Metheun & Co. Ltd.

Cresswell, T. (1996) *In Place/Out of Place: Ideology, Difference and Transgression*. London: Routledge.

Crow, L. (1996) *Including All Our Lives: Renewing the Social Model of Disability*. California: The Women's Press.

Davidson, J. (2000) 'The world was getting smaller: women, agoraphobia, and bodily boundaries.' *Area 32*, 31–40.

Davidson, J. (2008) 'Autistic culture online: virtual communication and cultural expression on the spectrum.' *Social and Cultural Geography 9*, 7, 791–806.

Davidson, J. and Smith, M. (2009) 'Autistic autobiographies and more than human emotional geographies.' *Environment and Planning D: Society and Space 27*, 898–916.

Davis, K. K., Davis, J. S. and Dowler, L. (2004) 'In motion, and out of place: The public space(s) of Tourette Syndrome.' *Social Science and Medicine 59*, 103–112.

Davis, T. (1995) 'The Diversity of Queer Politics and the Redefinition of Sexual Identity and Community in Urban Spaces.' In D. Bell and G. Valentine (eds) *Mapping Desire: Geographies of Sexuality*. London: Routledge.

Dear, M., Gaber, L. and Takahashi, L. (1999) 'Seeing people differently: The socio-spatial construction of disability.' *Environment and Planning D: Society and Space 15*, 455–480.

Domosh, M. (1998) 'Geography and gender: Home, again?' *Progress in Human Geography 22*, 276–282.

Drew, P. and Wootton, A. (eds) (1988) *Erving Goffman: Exploring the Interaction Order*. Cambridge: Polity Press.

Duncan, A. and Ley, D. (eds) (1993) *Place/Culture/Representation*. London: Routledge.

Dunn, W. (2007) 'Ecology of Human Performance Model.' In S. Dunbar (ed.) *Occupational Therapy Models for Intervention with Children and Families*. Thorofare, NJ: Slack Inc., pp.127–156.

Dunn, W., Myles, B. and Orr, S. (2002) 'Sensory processing issues associated with Asperger syndrome: A preliminary investigation.' *American Journal of Occupational Therapy 56*, 97–102.

Dunn, W., Saiter, J. and Rinner, L. (2002) 'Asperger Syndrome and sensory processing: A conceptual model and guidance for intervention planning.' *Focus on Autism and Other Developmental Disabilities 13*, 3, 172–185.

Dyck, I. (1995) 'Hidden geographies: The changing lifeworlds of women with disabilities.' *Social Science and Medicine 40*, 307–320.

Dyck, I. (2003) 'Feminism and Health Geography: Twin tracks or divergent agendas?' *Gender, Place and Culture 10*, 4, 361–368.

Dyck, I. and O'Brien, P. (2003) 'Thinking about environment: Incorporating geographies of disability into rehabilitation science.' *The Canadian Geographer 47*, 4, 400–413.

Edmonds, G. (ed.) (2008) *Asperger Syndrome and Social Relationships: Adults Speak Out About Asperger Syndrome.* London: Jessica Kingsley Publishers.

Ehlers, S. and Gillberg, C. (1993) 'The epidemiology of Asperger Syndrome. A total population study.' *Journal of Child Psychology and Psychiatry 34,* 8, 1327–1350.

Eyles, J. (1985) *Senses of Place.* Cheshire: Silverbrook Press.

Fitzpatrick, M. (2008) *Defeating Autism: A Damaging Delusion.* London: Routledge.

Fombonne, E. (2005) 'The changing epidemiology of autism.' *Journal of Applied Research in Intellectual Disabilities 18,* 281–294.

Frith, U. (1991) *Autism and Asperger Syndrome.* Cambridge: Cambridge University Press.

Frith, U. (2004) 'Emanuel Miller lecture: Confusions and controversies about Asperger Syndrome.' *Journal of Child Psychology and Psychiatry 45,* 672–686.

Gardner, C. B. (1991) 'Stigma and the public self: Notes on communication, self and others.' *Journal of Contemporary Ethnography 20,* 251–262.

Gaus, V. (2007) *Cognitive Behaviour Therapy for Adult Asperger Syndrome.* New York: Guilford Press.

Gerland, G. (1996) *A Real Person.* London: Souvenir Press.

Ghaziuddin, M. (2005) *Mental Health Aspects of Autism and Asperger Syndrome.* London: Jessica Kingsley Publishers.

Goffman, E. (1959) *The Presentation of Self in Everyday Life.* New York: Penguin.

Goffman, E. (1967) *Interaction Ritual.* London: Cox and Wyman.

Golledge, R. G. (1991) 'Tactual strip maps as navigational aids.' *Journal of Visual Impairments and Blindness 85,* 7, 296–301.

Gowen, E. and Miall, C. (2005) 'Behavioural aspects of cerebellar function in adults with Aspergers Syndrome.' *The Cerebellum 4,* 279–289.

Gray, C. (2004) 'Grays guide to bullying parts I–III.' *The Morning News 16,* 1–60.

Gregson, N. and Rose, G. (2000) 'Taking Butler elsewhere: Performativities, spatialities and subjectivities.' *Environment and Planning D: Society and Space 18,* 433–452.

Gurney, C. (1990) 'The meaning of the home in the decade of owner occupation.' *School for Advanced Urban Studies 88.* Bristol: University of Bristol Saus Publications.

Habermas, J. (1962) *The Structural Transformation of the Public Sphere: An Inquiry into a Category of Bourgeois Society.* Cambridge, MA: The MIT Press.

Hall, K. (2001) *Asperger Syndrome, the Universe and Everything.* London: Jessica Kingsley Publishers.

Heidegger, M. (1962) *Being and Time.* New York: Harper & Row.

Hewetson, A. (2002) *The Stolen Child: Aspects of Autism and Aspergers Syndrome.* Westport, CT: Bergin & Garvey.

Honda, H., Shimizu, Y. and Rutter, M. (2005) 'No effect of MMR withdrawal on the incidence of autism: A total population study.' *Journal of Child Psychology and Psychiatry 46*, 572–579.

Horowitz, A. V. (2002) *Creating Mental Illness.* Chicago, IL: University of Chicago Press.

Howlin, P. (1997) *Autism and Asperger Syndrome: Preparing for Adulthood.* New York: Routledge.

Hume, D. (1739) *A Treatise of Human Nature,* edited by L. A. Selby-Bigge, 2nd edition revised by P. H. Nidditch. Oxford: Clarendon Press, 1975.

Hume, D. (1758) *An Enquiry Concerning Human Understanding, in Enquiries Concerning Human Understanding and Concerning the Principles of Morals,* edited by L. A. Selby-Bigge, 3rd edition revised by P. H. Nidditch. Oxford: Clarendon Press, 1975.

Husserl, E. (1970) *The Crisis of European Sciences and Transcendental Phenomenology.* Evanston, IL: Northwestern University Press.

Illich, I. (1990) *Limits to Medicine.* London: Penguin.

Illouz, E. (2008) *Saving the Modern Soul: Therapy, Emotions and the Culture of Self Help.* Berkeley, CA: University of California Press.

Imrie, R. (1996) *Disability and the City: International Perspectives.* London: Paul Chapman Publishing.

Johnson, J., Cohen, P., Kasen, S. and Brook, J. (2007) 'Extensive television viewing and the development of attention and learning difficulties during adolescence.' Archives of Pediatrics and Adolescent Medicine 161, 5, 480–486.

Imrie, R. (2001) 'Barriered and bounded places and the spatialities of disability.' *Urban Studies 38*, 231–237.

Jordan, R. (1999) *Autistic Spectrum Disorders: An Introductory Handbook for Practitioners.* London: David Fulton Publishers Limited.

Jurecic, A. (2007) 'Neurodiversity.' *College English 69*, 5, 421–442.

Kanner, L. (1943) 'Autistic disturbances of affective contact.' *Nervous Child 2*, 217–250.

Kendall, C. (2009) *Asperger's Syndrome Guide for Teens and Young Adults: Thriving (Not Just Surviving).* California: Visions Research.

Kenway, I. (2009) 'Blessing or curse? Autism and the rise of the internet.' *Journal of Religion, Disability and Health 13*, 2, 94–103.

Kim, Y. S., Koh, Y. J. and Levanthal, B. (2005) 'School bullying and suicidal risk in Korean middle school students.' *Pediatrics 115*, 357–363.

Kitchin, R. and Lysaght, K. (2003) 'Heterosexism and the geographies of everyday life in Belfast, Northern Ireland.' *Environment and Planning A* *35*, 489–510.

Koegel, L. and La Zebnik, C. (2009) *Growing Up on the Spectrum: A Guide to Life, Love and Learning for Teens and Young Adults with Autism and Asperger's.* London: Penguin.

Lane, C. (2007) *Shyness: How Normal Behaviour Became a Sickness.* London: Yale University Press.

Lefebvre, H. (1991) *The Production of Space.* Oxford: Blackwell.

Lewin, F. (2001) 'The meaning of home amongst elderly immigrants: directions for future research and theoretical development.' *Housing Studies 16*, 3, 353–370.

Little, L. (2001) 'Peer victimization of children with Asperger Spectrum Disorders.' *Journal of the American Academy of Child and Adolescent Psychiatry Volume 40*, 995–996.

Little, L. (2002) 'Middle class mothers' perception of peer and sibling victimization among children with Asperger's Syndrome and nonverbal learning disorders.' *Issues in Comprehensive Paediatric Nursing 25*, 43–57.

Lord, C. and Bishop, S'. (2010) 'Autism Spectrum Disorders: Diagnosis, prevalence, and services for children and families.' *Sharing Child and Youth Development Knowledge 24*, 2, 1–21.

Lovett, A. A. and Gattrell, A. C. (1988) 'The geography of Spina Bifida in England and Wales.' *Transactions of the Institute of British Geographers 13*, 288–302.

Lovett, J. P. (2005) *Solutions for Adults with Asperger Syndrome: Maximizing the Benefits, Minimizing the Drawbacks to Achieve Success.* Gloucester, MA: Fair Winds Press.

Lustbader, W. and Hooyman, N. (2004) *Taking Care of Aging Family Members: A Practical Guide.* New York: Free Press.

Madriaga, M. (2010) 'I avoid pubs and the student union like the plague: Students with Asperger Syndrome and their negotiation of university spaces.' *Children's Geographies, 8*, 1, 39–50.

Marris, P. (1974) *Loss and Change.* London: Routledge.

Mayer, D. (1981) 'Geographical clues about multiple sclerosis.' *Annals of the Association of American Geographers 71*, 1, 28–39.

Mayes, S. D., Calhoun, S. L. and Crites, D. L. (2001) 'Does DSM-IV Asperger's disorder exist?' *Journal of Abnormal Child Psychology 29*, 3, 263–271.

McDowell, L. (1999) *A Feminist Glossary of Human Geography.* London: Arnold.

McGrath, L., Reavey, P. and Brown, S. D. (2008) 'The scenes and spaces of anxiety: embodied expressions of distress in public and private fora.' *Emotion, Space and Society 1*, 56–64.

McKean, T. A. (1998) 'A Personal Account of Autism.' In E. Schopler and G. B. Mesibov (eds) *Asperger Syndrome or High Functioning Autism?* New York: Plenum, 345–356.

McKelvey, J. R., Lambert, R., Mottron, L. and Shevell, M. I. (1995) 'Right hemisphere dysfunction in Aspergers Syndrome.' *Journal of Child Neurology 10*, 4, 310–314.

Merlau Ponty, M. (1962) *Phenomenology of Perception*, trans. by Colin Smith. New York: Humanities Press, 1962; London: Routledge & Kegan Paul, 1962; translation revised by Forrest Williams, 1981; reprinted 2002.

Merlau Ponty, M. (1963) *The Structure of Behaviour*, trans. by Alden Fisher. Boston: Beacon Press, 1963.

Meyer, L., Park, H., Grenot Scheyer, M., Schwartz, I. and Harry, B. (1998) 'Participatory research: New approaches to the research to practice dilemma.' *Journal of the Association for Persons with Severe Handicaps 23*, 165–177.

Misztal, B. (2001) 'Normality and trust in Goffman's theory of interaction order.' *Sociological Theory 19*, 3, 312–324.

Molloy, H. and Vasil, L. (2002) 'The social construction of Asperger's Syndrome: the pathologising of difference?' *Disability & Society, 17*, 6, 659–669.

Morris, J. (ed.) (1996) *Encounters With Strangers: Feminism and Disability*. London: Women's Press.

Morris, J. (1998) *Don't Leave Us Out*. York: Joseph Rowntree Foundation.

Muller, E., Schuler, A. and Yates, G. B. (2008) 'Social challenges and supports from the perspective of individuals with Asperger Syndrome and other autism spectrum disabilities.' *Autism 12*, 2, 173–190.

Oliver, M. (1990) *The Politics of Disablement*. London: Macmillan Press.

Oliver, M. (1996) *Understanding Disability: From Theory to Practice*. London: Macmillan.

O'Moore, A. M. and Hillery, B. (1991) 'What Do Teachers Need to Know?' In M. Elliott (ed.) *Bullying: A Practical Guide to Coping in Schools*. Harlow: David Fulton, pp.56–69.

Olweus, D. (1993) *Bullying at School: What We Know and What We Can Do*. Cambridge, MA: Blackwell.

Parr, H. (1999) 'Bodies and Psychiatric Medicine: Interpreting Different Geographies of Mental Health.' In R. Butler and H. Parr (eds) *Mind and Body Spaces*. London: Routledge.

Parr, H. (2000) 'Interpreting the hidden social geographies of mental health: Ethnographies of inclusion and exclusion in semi institutional places.' *Health and Place 6*, 225–237.

Parr, H. (2008) *Mental Health and Social Space: Towards Inclusionary Geographies*. London: Blackwell Publishing.

Parr, H., Philo, C. and Burns, N. (2004) 'Social geographies of rural mental health: Experiencing inclusions and exclusions.' *Institute of British Geographers 29*, 401–419.

Payer, L. (1992) *Diseasemongers*. New York: John Wiley.

Philo, C. and Wolch, J. (2001) 'The "three waves" of research in mental health geography: A review and critical commentary.' *Epidemiologia e Psichiatria Sociale 10*, 230–244.

Pilcher, J. and Whelehan, I. (2004) *50 Key Concepts in Gender Studies*. California: Sage Publications.

Pilgrim, D. and Bentall, R. (1999) 'The medicalisation of misery: A critical realist analysis of the concept of depression.' *Journal of Mental Health 8*, 3, 261–274.

Portway, S. and Johnson, B. (2003) 'Asperger Syndrome and the children who "don't quite fit in".' *Early Child Development and Care 173*, 4, 435–443.

Preece, D. (2002) 'Consultation with children with autistic spectrum disorders about their experience of short term residential care.' *British Journal of Learning Disabilities 30*, 97–104.

Priestly, M. (2003) *Disability: A Life Course Approach*. London: Polity Press.

Rhode, M. and Klauber, T. (eds) (2004) *The Many Faces of Asperger's Syndrome*. London: H. Karnac Books Ltd.

Rogers, A. and Pilgrim, D. (2003) *Mental Health and Inequality*. London: Palgrave Macmillan.

Roth, I. (2010) *The Autism Spectrum in the 21st Century: Exploring Psychology, Biology and Practice*. London: Jessica Kingsley Publishers.

Roth, M. and Gillis, J. (2014) 'Convenience with the click of a mouse: A survey of adults with Autism Spectrum Disorder on online dating.' *Sexuality and Disability 33*, 1, 133–150.

Ruddick, S. M. (1996) *Young and Homeless in Hollywood: Mapping Social Identities*. New York: Routledge.

Ryan, S. (2005) 'People don't do odd, do they? Mothers making sense of the reactions of others towards their learning disabled children in public places.' *Children's Geographies 3*, 3, 291–305.

Ryan, S. and Raisanen, U. (2008) 'It's like you are just a spectator in this thing: Experiencing social life the "aspie" way.' *Emotion, Space and Society 1*, 135–143.

Safran, J. S. (2002) 'Supporting students with Asperger's Syndrome in general education.' *Teaching Exceptional Children 67*, 2, 151–160.

Sarantakos, S. (2005) *Social Research*. New York: Palgrave Macmillan.

Saunders, P. (1989) 'The meaning of home in contemporary English culture.' *Housing Studies 4*, 3, 177–192.

Schneider, E. (2002) *Living the Good Life with Autism*. London: Jessica Kingsley Publishers.

Schneider, G. E. (1969) 'Two visual systems.' *Science 163*, 3870, 895–902.

Scholte, R. H. J., De Kemp, R. A., Haselager, G. J. and Engels, R. (2007) 'Longitudinal stability in bullying and victimisation in childhood and adolescence.' *Journal of Abnormal Child Psychology 35*, 217–238.

Schutz, A. (1962) *Collected Papers Vol 1. The Problem of Social Reality*. Nijhoff: Martinus.

Simmons, J. (2002) *Crime in England and Wales 2001/2002*. London: Home Office.

Singer, J. (1999) 'Why Can't You Be Normal for Once in Your Life? From a Problem with No Name to the Emergence of a New Category of Difference.' In M. Corker and S. French (eds) *Disability Discourse*. Buckingham: OU Press.

Smith, P. K. and Sharp, S. (1994) *School Bullying: Insights and Perspectives*. London: Routledge.

Smith-Myles, B., Tapscott Cook, K., Miller, N., Rinner, L. and Robbins, L. (2000) *Asperger Syndrome and Sensory Issues. Practical Solutions for Making Sense of the World*. Shawnee Mission, Kansas: Autism, Asperger Publishing Company.

Tamimi, S. (2002) *Pathological Child Psychiatry and the Medicalisation of Childhood*. London: Routledge.

Teather, E. (ed.) (1999) *Embodied Geographies: Spaces, Bodies and Rites of Passage*. London: Routledge.

Tonkiss, F. (2005) *Space, the City and Social Theory: Social Relations and Urban Forms*. Cambridge: Polity Press.

Toomey, D. (1996) 'The dark side of parental involvement in education.' *Forum on Education 51*, 60–72.

Tuan, Y. F. (2004) 'Home.' In S. Harrison, S. Pile and N. Thrift (eds) *Patterned Ground: The Entanglements of Nature and Culture*. London: Reaktion Books.

UPIAS (1976) *Fundamental Principles of Disability*. London: Union of the Physically Impaired Against Segregation/The Disability Alliance.

Wakefield, A. J., Murch, S. H., Anthony, A., Linnel, J. *et al.* (1998) 'Ileal-lymphoid-nodular hyperplasia, non specific colitis, and pervasive development disorder in children.' *The Lancet 351*, 637–641.

Walmsley, D. J. and Lewis, G. J. (1984) *Human Geography: Behavioural Approaches*. Essex: Longman Group Limited.

Walsh, P. (2010) 'Asperger Syndrome and the supposed obligation not to bring disabled lives into the world.' *Journal of Medical Ethics 36*, 521–524.

Ward, L. (1997) *Seen and Heard: Involving Disabled Children and Young People in Research and Development Projects*. York: Joseph Rowntree Foundation.

Williams, D. (1996) *Autism – An Inside Out Approach*. London: Jessica Kingsley Publishers.

Williams, D. (2005) *Autism: An Inside-Out Approach: An Innovative Look at the Mechanics of Autism and its Developmental Cousins.* London and Philadelphia: Jessica Kingsley Publishers.

Wing, L. (1981) *Asperger's Syndrome: A Clinical Account.* London: National Autistic Society.

Wing, L. and Gould, J. (1979) 'Severe impairments of social interaction and associated abnormalities in children: Epidemiology and classification.' *Journal of Autism and Developmental Disorders 9*, 11–29.

Young, I. M. (1990) *Justice and the Politics of Difference.* Princeton: Princeton University Press.

INDEX

Gazzaniga, M.S. 32, 37
Gerland, G.41, 85
Gillis, J. 122
Goddard, L. 41, 63
Goffman, E. 72
Grandin, T. 17, 41, 50, 53, 85, 159, 160
Griffiths, M.D. 149

Hall, E. 45
Hall, S. 72
Hanschu, B. 44
Haq, I. 72
hearing
  description of 30–1
  differences for people with ASD 45–6
  and echoic memory 37
  in schools 75
Heatherington, T. 32, 37
Henault, I. 125
Higashida, N. 64
Hock, R.R. 29
Hofmann, S.G. 117
Holliday Willey, J. 72, 106
home
  children with ASD at 112–16
  experiences of for people with ASD 105–12
  sharing space at 108–9
Hunt, N. 149
Hyman, S.L. 48
hyper-sensitivity
  description of 42, 43
  in school 80–1
hypo-sensitivity
  description of 42, 43
  and sensory-seeking behaviours 44

iconic memory 37, 61
implicit memory 62
internet see cyber space

Jessell, T.M. 25
job interviews 92–5
Johnson, J. 149

Kandel, E.R. 25
Kasari, C. 72
Kemner, C. 59
Kerkhof, P. 150
Kinnealey, M. 56
Kitchin, R. 72
Klin, A. 140
Koenig, K. 56
Kuhanek, H.M. 43
Kuschner, E.S. 48

Lane, A.E. 44
language
  of autism 13–15
  and memory 36
Le Couteur, A. 72
learning
  role of memory in 37–8
learning plans 76–81
lighting in schools 74–5
long-term memory 36, 62

Marks, L.E. 60
Mayes, S. 41
Mazurek, M. 149
Meerkerk, G.J. 149
Melzack, R. 33
memory
  role in learning 37–8
  and sensory systems 35–8
  types of 36–7, 61–3
Mildner, V. 39
Miller, L.J. 25
Mitchell, P. 139
modalities 23–4
Moloney, P. 72
Morahan-Martin, J. 150
Mottron, L. 157
Murphy, L. 48

The Guide to Good Mental Health on the Autism Spectrum

Jeanette Purkis, Emma Goodall and Jane Nugent

Forewords by Wenn Lawson and Kirsty Dempster-Rivett

Paperback: £14.99 / $24.95
ISBN: 978 1 84905 670 0
eISBN: 978 1 78450 1952
272 pages

Filled with strategies and advice, this empowering guide presents practical ways to improve the mental wellbeing of people on the Autism Spectrum.

This helpful guide focusses on the specific difficulties that can arise for people on the autism spectrum who may also experience a mental illness. The book includes information on common mental health issues, such as depression and anxiety, as well as strategies for improving sleep patterns and mindfulness. Providing guidance on the benefits and drawbacks of therapy pets, medication, and psychotherapy, the authors offer balanced perspectives on treatment options and introduce self-help strategies tailored to meet your needs and improve your mental wellbeing. A number of short personal narratives from people on the autism spectrum and mental health issues illustrate the text.

The book also includes a list of resources, books and organisations that can provide further support and inspiration.

Jeanette Purkis has a lived experience of autism and mental illness and is also the author of two books looking at aspects of autism. She holds a Master's degree in Fine Arts from RMIT University and works full-time in the Australian Public Service. Jeanette lives in Canberra, Australia.

Dr Emma Goodall has Asperger's syndrome and has had professional experience of mental health services. She has a PhD in the area of education and the autism spectrum and is the author of a text book for teaching AS children. Emma is a Senior Autism Advisor in South Australia and an executive committee member of the Australian Society for Autism Research (ASfAR), as well as an executive committee member for the Autistic Self-Advocacy

Network (ASAN) of Australia and New Zealand. She lives in Adelaide, South Australia, with her partner.

Dr Jane Nugent is a Psychiatric Career Medical Officer with General Practitioner training. She has a special interest in mental health and a passion for psychopharmacology. She has a talent for taking highly technical information and making it accessible to non-specialists. Jane has been involved in pharmacology teaching for a variety of New Zealand and Australian institutions since 1997.

Unemployed on the Autism Spectrum
How to Cope with the Effects of Unemployment
and Jobhunt withConfidence
Michael John Carley
Foreword by Brenda Smith Myles, Ed.D.

Paperback: £12.99 / $19.95
ISBN: 978 1 84905 729 5
eISBN: 978 1 78450 158 7
160 pages

Unemployment can be an isolating experience. In this much-needed book, Michael John Carley reassures readers who are unemployed and have Autism Spectrum Disorder (ASD) that they are not alone.

Offering guidance on how you can cope with unemployment in a constructive and emotionally healthy manner, Michael John Carley writes with a crucial understanding of the isolation and negative emotions that unemployment can bring about if you have ASD. He explains why so many people find themselves out of work and how it's often not their fault. Providing guidance on how to maintain your confidence and motivation, this book offers advice on how you can pursue other opportunities, such as part-time work or volunteering. The book also features advice on how to manage your finances during periods of unemployment.

Michael John Carley is the Founder and former Executive Director of GRASP, the largest organization comprised of adults on the autism spectrum. As the Executive Director of ASTEP, he spoke at conferences focusing on Human Resources, Corporate Diversity & Inclusion, and he conducted numerous training events and webinars for individual Fortune 1000 companies. He lives with his wife and two sons in Green Bay, Wisconsin, where he now works as a School Consultant.

Sensory Perceptual Issues in Autism and Asperger Syndrome,
Different Sensory Experiences – Different Perceptual Worlds
Second Edition
Olga Bogdashina
Foreword by Manuel F. Casanova

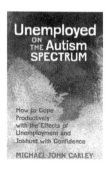

Paperback: £16.99 / $32.95
ISBN: 978 1 84905 673 1
eISBN: 978 1 78450 179 2
288 pages

Completely revised and updated, this book focuses on sensory perceptual problems as identified by individuals on the autism spectrum.

Despite frequently being identified by individuals with autism as one of the main problems they face, sensory perceptual issues are still often overlooked by professionals. The author covers the sensory perceptual experiences and sensitivities seen in autism spectrum conditions, and the cognitive differences caused by them. She considers assessment and intervention, and makes practical recommendations for selecting appropriate methods and techniques to eliminate sensory perceptual problems and enhance individual strengths.

Brought up-to-date with current research and the latest thinking on autism, this book enables teachers, parents, professionals and individuals with autism fully to understand and address the problematic aspects of the sensory perceptual differences of people with autism spectrum conditions.

Olga Bogdashina, MA, PhD, is Co-founder, Programme Leader and Lecturer at the UK branch of the International Autism Institute and Associate Consultant (Autism) to the European Institute of Child Education and Psychology (ICEP Europe). She has worked extensively in the field of autism as a teacher, lecturer and researcher, with a particular interest in sensory-perceptual and communication problems. Since 1994, she has been Director of the first day centre for children with autism in Ukraine and President of the Autism Society of Ukraine. She is the author of Autism and Spirituality, Autism and the Edges of the Known World, Theory of Mind and the Triad of Perspectives on Autism and Asperger Syndrome and Communication Issues in Autism and Asperger Syndrome, all published by Jessica Kingsley Publishers. Olga has an adult son with autism and lives in West Yorkshire, UK.